WORLD HISTORY

World War I

Robert Green

LUCENT BOOKS

An imprint of Thomson Gale, a part of The Thomson Corporation

Detroit • New York • San Francisco • New Haven, Conn. • Waterville, Maine • London

THOMSON

✦ ™

GALE

For my niece and nephews—Katie, Jordan, Ryan and Andrew.

© 2008 Thomson Gale, a part of The Thomson Corporation.

Thomson and Star Logo are trademarks and Gale and Lucent Books are registered trademarks used herein under license.

For more information, contact
Lucent Books
27500 Drake Rd.
Farmington Hills, MI 48331-3535
Or you can visit our Internet site at http://www.gale.com

LIBRARY OF CONGRESS CATALOGING-IN-PUBLICATION DATA

Green, Robert, 1969–
World War I / by Robert Green.
    p. cm. — (World history series)
Includes bibliographical references and index.
ISBN 978-1-4205-0025-7 (hardcover)
1. World War, 1914-1918. I. Title. II. Title: World War One. III. Title: World War 1.
D521.G755 2007
940.3—dc22

        2007024058

ISBN-10: 1-4205-0025-2

Printed in the United States of America

Contents

Foreword

Each year, on the first day of school, nearly every history teacher faces the task of explaining why his or her students should study history. Many reasons have been given. One is that lessons exist in the past from which contemporary society can benefit and learn. Another is that exploration of the past allows us to see the origins of our customs, ideas, and institutions. Concepts such as democracy, ethnic conflict, or even things as trivial as fashion or mores, have historical roots.

Reasons such as these impress few students, however. If anything, these explanations seem remote and dull to young minds. Yet history is anything but dull. And therein lies what is perhaps the most compelling reason for studying history: History is filled with great stories. The classic themes of literature and drama—love and sacrifice, hatred and revenge, injustice and betrayal, adversity and overcoming adversity—fill the pages of history books, feeding the imagination as well as any of the great works of fiction do.

The story of the Children's Crusade, for example, is one of the most tragic in history. In 1212 Crusader fever hit Europe. A call went out from the pope that all good Christians should journey to Jerusalem to drive out the hated Muslims and return the city to Christian control. Heeding the call, thousands of children made the journey. Parents bravely allowed many children to go, and entire communities were inspired by the faith of these small Crusaders. Unfortunately, many boarded ships captained by slave traders, who enthusiastically sold the children into slavery as soon as they arrived at their destination. Thousands died from disease, exposure, and starvation on the long march across Europe to the Mediterranean Sea. Others perished at sea.

Another story, from a modern and more familiar place, offers a soul-wrenching view of personal humiliation but also the ability to rise above it. Hatsuye Egami was one of 110,000 Japanese Americans sent to internment camps during World War II. "Since yesterday we Japanese have ceased to be human beings," he wrote in his diary. "We are numbers. We are no longer Egamis, but the number 23324. A tag with that number is on every trunk, suitcase and bag. Tags, also, on our breasts." Despite such dehumanizing treatment, most internees worked hard to control their bitterness. They created workable communities inside the camps and demonstrated again and again their loyalty as Americans.

These are but two of the many stories from history that can be found in the pages of the Lucent Books World History series. All World History titles rely on sound research and verifiable evidence, and all give students a clear sense of time, place, and chronology through maps and timelines as well as text.

All titles include a wide range of authoritative perspectives that demonstrate the complexity of historical interpretation and sharpen the reader's critical thinking skills. Formally documented quotations and annotated bibliographies enable students to locate and evaluate sources, often instantaneously via the Internet, and serve as valuable tools for further research and debate.

Finally, Lucent's World History titles present rousing good stories, featuring vivid primary source quotations drawn from unique, sometimes obscure sources such as diaries, public records, and contemporary chronicles. In this way, the voices of participants and witnesses as well as important biographers and historians bring the study of history to life. As we are caught up in the lives of others, we are reminded that we too are characters in the ongoing human saga, and we are better prepared for our own roles.

1914
World War I begins on July 28; the Panama Canal opens, shortening sea travel between the Atlantic and the Pacific.

1910	1915	1916	19

1915
Alexander Graham Bell, inventor of the telephone, makes the first transcontinental phone call, between New York and San Francisco; American film director D.W. Griffith premieres *The Birth of a Nation*, his silent epic about the American Civil War.

1916
James Joyce publishes *A Portra of the Artist as a Young Man*; U.S. general John J. Pershing leads U.S. troops into Mexico to search for Panch Villa; during the Easter Rebellion in Ireland, Irish nationalists try to overthrow British rule.

1918
Armistice signed between Allied and Central Powers, ending the fighting of World War I; an outbreak of Spanish influenza kills millions of people; daylight savings time is officially adopted in the United States.

1918   1919   1920

1917
The United States abandons neutrality and joins the Allied Powers fighting in World War I; the czars, or hereditary rulers of Russia, are overthrown in the Russian Revolution; women march on the White House to gain votes for American women.

1919
The British army guns down unarmed civilians in the town of Amritsar, India, leading for more calls for the end of British rule in India; the Treaty of Versailles is signed on June 28, formally ending World War I.

The Reason Why

Worild War I is near enough in time for us to answer many of the what, when, and where questions essential to understanding any historical event. Official records are available by the pile. Soldiers from all armies left accounts not only of the battles but also of their personal experiences in the fighting. Scholars have filled volumes of explanations on the doings of the war, so that nearly every day of the conflict is recorded in one manner or another. And photography, invented in the nineteenth century, was advanced enough and cameras common enough that we can even see what the soldiers and the battlefields looked like. The nagging question remains the why.

The immediate cause of the war was the assassination of Archduke Franz Ferdinand, heir to the throne of the Central European power of Austria-Hungary. The archduke was assassinated in Sarajevo, the traditional capital of Bosnia and Herzegovina and the largest city in an area of Europe known as the Balkans. In 1914 the area was ruled by Austria-Hungary—an empire now vanished. The assassin, Gavrilo Princip, a Bosnian Serb, and his coconspirators belonged to an underground movement that struggled for independence from the Austro-Hungarian Empire.

The assassination might have remained a contained incident, but it did not. It drew in one nation after another. Even as the great powers of Europe—Britain, France, and Russia on the one side, Germany and Austria-Hungary on the other—said they wanted only peace, they prepared for war. Europe became the epicenter of a political earthquake, and the shock waves spread quickly outward, reaching all the corners of the earth. It was a conflict that would be known to history as World War I, or the First World War.

Part of the continuing fascination with understanding why the war began arises from this global scale. There were few nations that the war failed to touch. It made people realize more than ever before that the world was interconnected—and that there was no escape from world events. It was a war that presented the unusual sight of Japanese warships protecting Allied convoys in the Mediterranean, Chinese laborers working behind Allied lines in France, Australians and New Zealanders fighting on Turkish soil, and starting in 1917, Americans fighting in trenches in Europe despite the American desire to remain neutral. In Africa, colonial forces from both the Allied and the Central Powers clashed, and African soldiers were enlisted to fight on both sides.

All this happened, moreover, at a time when much of the world looked favorably upon European civilization. China, the world's most populous country, had overthrown its emperor and founded a republic along Western democratic lines in 1912. Japan had succeeded in turning

Nineteen-year-old assassin Gavrilo Princip (second from right) resists arrest after killing Archduke Franz Ferdinand, heir to the Austro-Hungarian throne.

itself into a world-class commercial and military power in the late eighteenth and early nineteenth centuries by using Western scientific methods. European colonial governors ruled the subcontinent of India and much of the continent of Africa, slowly modernizing those nations and promising eventual self-rule under local democratic governments. Everywhere, it seemed, the West was triumphant.

Spiraling Out of Control

Just why then would the countries of Europe throw themselves into a brutal war that killed millions and undercut faith in Europe as a center of civilization? Two common explanations for the outbreak of World War I are that it occurred more or less accidentally and that the arms race that preceded the war led to war itself. These two ideas are connected. The arms race, in which all the major powers of Europe engaged in the years before 1914, created an explosive atmosphere, which broke into hostilities with the assassination of Archduke Franz Ferdinand.

Perhaps the best expression of this theory comes from Sir Edward Grey, Britain's foreign secretary during World War I. In 1925 Grey bleakly concluded that by engaging in an arms race a nation risks setting ablaze the conflict it seeks to deter:

Great armaments lead inevitably to war. If there are armaments on one side, there must be armaments on other sides. The increase of armaments produces a consciousness of the strength of other nations and a sense of fear. Fear begets suspicion and distrust and evil imaginings of all sorts, till . . . every government regards every precaution of every other government as evidence of hostile intent. . . . The enormous growth of armaments in Europe, the sense of insecurity and fear caused by them—it was these that made war inevitable.[1]

New Assessments

That inevitability of war in 1914 has since been challenged, especially by German scholars studying Germany's ambitions in the run up to the war. These scholars take a much darker view of humanity. They place the blame for the war squarely on the shoulders of Germany. "Nations do not launch wars because they are afraid," wrote one scholar, "but because they are confident that they will gain more by resorting to force than by refraining from doing so. This was true no less in 1914 than in other cases."[2]

Indeed, those who knew the German kaiser Wilhelm before the war believed that his ambition took Germany and the rest of the world into battle. His uncle, the heir to the British throne and future King Edward VII, concluded simply that "Willy is a bully."[3] And by 1909, after a visit to Germany, King Edward VII remarked: "We may safely look upon Germany as our bitterest foe, as she hardly attempts to conceal it."[4]

Winston Churchill, who was to play such a large role in the First and Second World Wars, takes a more subtle view,

Kaiser Wilhelm II in 1896, eight years after being crowned emperor of Germany.

placing blame on Germany but also on the uncontrollable events of history. "Events also got on to certain lines, and no one could get them off again," he wrote. "Germany clanked obstinately, recklessly, awkwardly towards the crater and dragged us all in with her."[5]

The question of why war broke out in 1914 has so fascinated historians, in part, because the answers say much about the nature of warfare and of the people who make war, and perhaps lend some clues to preventing war in the future. This book provides an introduction to the what, when, and where, leaving the why for the reader to decide. It is important to realize that in 1914 most soldiers knew little of the reason why, and they arrived on the battlefield singing, with a soldier's wry humor, their own answer to the question:

We're here because we're here

Because we're here, because we're here;

We're here because we're here

Because we're here, because we're here.[6]

Chapter One

The Western Front —the Center of the Storm

Although small countries such as Serbia and Belgium provided a stage for the opening days of World War I, the war was principally a struggle between the great powers of Europe—Germany, France, Great Britain, Russia, and the Austro-Hungarian Empire. Europe would provide the battlefields for the two greatest fronts in the war—the western front and the eastern front. The locations of these two fronts, or battle areas, are west and east of Germany.

Since the battlefields ranged over such a large area and continued to expand, it might be useful to remember where the center was. For although the storm would swirl over an ever greater area, drawing in many nations of the globe, the center of the storm was always Germany, and the principal front was the western front. What was so extraordinary about Germany that it could create such havoc throughout Europe and beyond?

Germany's Growing Appetite

The answer lies in Germany's rivalry with the other great powers of Europe. Although the Germans are an ancient people, the German nation was a relative newcomer to great nation status. The most populous nation of Europe today, Germany had only come into being as a modern political state in the nineteenth century. In the competitive atmosphere of nineteenth-century Europe, the Germans felt that they needed to establish Germany as a world power and an equal of Britain and France. And the Germans wanted to do it in a hurry. Germany did this both through diplomacy and war.

France, which shared a long border with Germany, was the target of both a diplomatic offensive and a military offensive. Alliances sought to isolate France in European politics, and a war in 1871 between Germany and France secured the continuing resentment of the

French toward their victorious German neighbors. At the end of the war, Germany proclaimed itself an empire. It also seized the French province of Alsace and part of Lorraine, reorganizing them as the German imperial province of Alsace-Lorraine. The loss of this territory to Germany provided a lasting injury to French national pride, and its recovery became a central war aim of France in World War I.

Germany also hoped to get hold of lands outside Europe, seeing the benefits of British and French colonies. France and Great Britain in 1914 ruled worldwide empires made up of these colonies. British and French colonies could be found from Africa to Southeast Asia and China and around the globe in the Caribbean. Some of their colonial holdings proved profitable and some cost a small fortune to rule. No matter what the financial situation was, the colonies earned for the two European powers prestige in world affairs. The two powers, in other words, exercised an influence out of proportion to the size of their

German troops edge out of their trenches to advance toward the enemy on the western front.

The Public Face of War

Horatio Herbert Kitchener became the public face of World War I in Great Britain. At the outbreak of hostilities, Kitchener was one of the few who predicted a long, bloody war. To fight the war, Britain would need to recruit many more soldiers for the army. Kitchener was made secretary of state for war in 1914 and was undoubtedly Britain's most famous soldier. His picture, with his long mustache and stern gaze, adorned recruiting posters, and Britain's large volunteer army became known as Kitchener's Army. Kitchener helped direct the course of the war, concentrating on overall strategy, at least until 1916.

In June 1916 Kitchener sailed on the HMS *Hampshire* on a diplomatic mission to Russia. The warship hit a mine left by a German U-boat near the Orkney Islands off the north coast of Scotland, depriving Great Britain of its most famous soldier.

home countries and their populations. Germany wanted for itself the same influence over foreign parts of the globe and the respect that foreign colonies had given its European rivals.

Aside from seizing land in Europe, Germany set about claiming colonies in other parts of the globe. France, Great Britain, and even little Belgium held overseas colonies, why not the Germans? The Germans carved off a part of China on the Shandong Peninsula, which included the city of Qingdao. Germany also secured colonial possessions in Africa, which was being rapidly conquered by European powers. German power thus continued to grow, and the Germans rapidly increased spending on arms to support the troops needed for conquest and war.

The other European powers reacted to the growth of German power with alarm

and suspicion. As the Germans raced to build a giant fleet of ships to rival the British—who as an island people had always relied on the navy for defense— and an army to match that of the French and Russians, other nations raced to keep up with them. Spending on arms skyrocketed. This European arms race pointed ominously toward war, and some historians would later credit this buildup of weapons and the suspicion that they drew in their wake as the real cause of World War I.

The Race for Arms

To calm the situation, Germany pursued a delicate diplomatic policy. Under the leadership of Otto von Bismarck, the chancellor, or leader, of Germany from 1871 to 1890, Germany attempted to keep good relations with Russia and with

Britain and even calm French fears. Bismarck, as the first chancellor of the German Empire, hoped to peacefully secure an overseas expansion for Germany and a dominant role in Europe. He worked closely in these aims with Wilhelm I, the emperor of the German Empire.

When Wilhelm II came to power in 1888, Bismarck found that the new kaiser, or emperor, was not interested in his cautious approach. In Wilhelm II, Germany had found an adventurous gambler who was determined to speed up the making of a large German Empire. He was willing to do this as much by war as by diplomacy. And once Bismarck had been pushed aside in 1890, the kaiser was free to adopt a more hostile stance both toward the Russians to the east and the French and their British allies to the west.

Wilhelm's impatience and irritation with Bismarck and his policies led the new emperor to take German policy into his own hands. He would rule his empire more directly, controlling its diplomacy on his own. So thoroughly did he take the reins of power that that era of German history is known as Wilhelmine Germany, or the Germany of Wilhelm.

In a sharp break from Bismarck's former strategy, Wilhelm's diplomacy relied on ultimatums to enemies and pledges of support for friends. Other nations would do what the German kaiser wanted or else face his wrath. Feeling itself increasingly closed in by enemies, Germany pushed for a war sooner than later. Count Helmuth von Moltke, the chief of the general staff, the highest military leader in Germany, had already urged the kaiser to strike before Germany's enemies became even stronger. All of Europe sensed that war was coming and that it would center upon the Germany of Wilhelm.

The "Iron Chancellor," Otto von Bismarck, in 1894.

The Balkan Crisis

The crisis in the Balkans that resulted from the assassination of the heir to the Austro-Hungarian throne provided just the opportunity for Wilhelm to make his war. The Austro-Hungarian Empire was the weak partner of Germany, and the kaiser pushed this ally into decisive action in the Balkans. Austria adopted the kaiser's favorite diplomatic initiative—the ultimatum. Austria's ultimatum required that the Serbian government take responsibility for the assassination and take quick steps to weed out hostile elements in its military. This was delivered to Serbia on July 23, 1914, and even when the Serbs attempted to meet the demands of the Austro-Hungarians, an invasion of Serbia was launched with the full backing of Germany. As expected, Russia as an ally of Serbia mobilized for war. In fact, all the armies of Europe sprang into action. The kaiser had his war, and the struggle for Europe could begin.

The German general staff had already provided detailed plans for the war based on the ideas of Count Alfred von Schlieffen, a former chief of the general staff. Schlieffen called for the invasion of France from the north. According to this plan, the armies of Germany would sweep through Belgium and into north-

German plans to invade France from the north were originally proposed by Prussian general Alfred von Schlieffen.

ern France, opening a wide front north of Paris. The armies would then turn southward and sweep toward the French capital. The Germans expected this thrust to defeat France in a matter of weeks, freeing German troops to turn east and face the Russians.

Even before Germany declared war on France on August 3, 1914, German troops had started moving into Belgium according to Schlieffen's plan. Most people expected the war to be a short one. "You will be home before the leaves have fallen from the trees,"[7] the kaiser told his troops in August. The British, who declared war after Germany's invasion of Belgium, believed the same. All in all, it was expected to be a short, glorious war for everyone.

The Opening Salvos

Belgium received an ultimatum from the kaiser to surrender at once or be destroyed, and when the Belgians refused, a million Germans marched into Belgium

At the beginning of World War I, the Schlieffen plan seemed to be working for the German army.

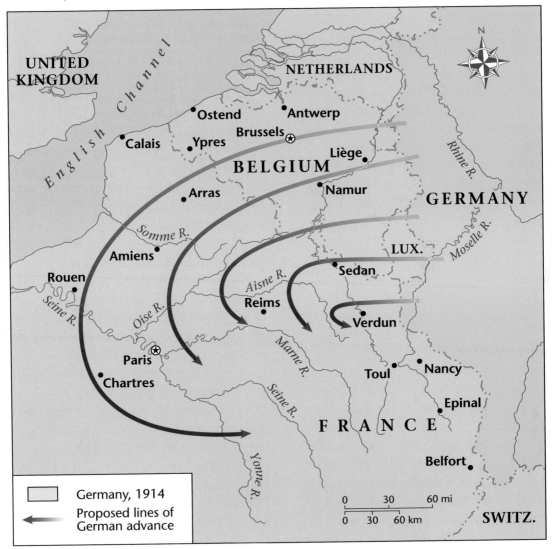

on August 4. German guns, notably the giant artillery pieces made by the Krupp works at the German city of Essen, pounded Belgian fortifications. The thunderous barrages shattered the stone fortresses, and German soldiers quickly swept through Belgium, leaving death and destruction in their path. Western newspapers soon began condemning this so-called rape of Belgium, and attitudes in Europe hardened against the invading Germans.

The invasion of Belgium and Luxembourg was contrary to international law, but the Germans felt that such legalities must be swept aside. Indeed, the Germans argued that they launched the invasion not out of choice but to prevent France from attacking Germany. German chancellor Theobald von Bethmann-Hollweg made this clear in a speech to the Reichstag, or German parliament, on August 4, 1914:

We are now in a state of necessity, and necessity knows no law. Our troops have occupied Luxemburg and perhaps are already on Belgian soil. Gentlemen, that is contrary to the dictates of international law. It is true that the French government has declared at Brussels that France is willing to respect the neutrality of Belgium, so long as her opponent respects it. We knew, however, that France stood ready for invasion. France could wait, but we could not wait. A French movement upon our flank upon the lower Rhine might have been disastrous. So we were

compelled to override the just protest of the Luxemburg and Belgian Governments.[8]

In his own speech to German soldiers on the way to the front, the kaiser rejoiced that that the Germans would finally have a chance to show their greatness in war: "Remember the German people are the chosen of God. On me, the German Emperor, the spirit of God has descended. I am His sword, His weapon and His vicegerent. Woe to the disobedient and death to cowards and unbelievers."[9]

When Germany attacked Belgium, the French reacted exactly as Schlieffen had expected. They threw a strong army into Alsace-Lorraine to recapture this former French territory. They were met, however, by strong German defenses and driven back. While the French thrust toward Germany, the Germans continued their advance through Belgium and southward into France itself.

Not only were the Germans well armed with their guns from the Krupp factory, but they were well organized and in good spirits. Support troops moved rapidly down the railways toward the battle front, and the French raced northward to check their advance. The Schlieffen Plan called for the German army to outflank the French defenders, and the two armies raced for good positioning. As the Germans wheeled south and began their advance toward Paris along a wide front, they met determined resistance by French and British troops.

The Defense of France

After much debate, Great Britain had declared war on Germany and sent the British Expeditionary Force to take up positions in northern France. The violation of Belgian neutrality, the possibility of the defeat of France, and the prospect of Germany controlling continental Europe prompted the British to form an allied front with France to stop the Germans. "Only a menace to the very life of the British nation would stir the British Empire from its placid and tolerant detachment from Continental affairs," wrote Winston Churchill, First Lord of the Admiralty, the chief of the British navy. "But that menace Germany was destined to supply."[10]

The British force under the command of Sir John French met the Germans for the first time in the Battle of Mons on August 23, 1914. The British took up defensive positions near the canal at the Belgian town of Mons and held off a German force more than double their numbers, though taking about sixteen hundred casualties over the next few days. As the French line continued to collapse around them, however, the British pulled back along with the French toward the Marne, a river east of Paris, which forms a natural defensive barrier.

In the initial days of the German attack, the Schlieffen Plan seemed to be working. Allied forces were forced to fight a rearguard action, while preventing the Germans from outflanking them to the north. The British and French settled into an area around the Marne to try to stop the German advance. Two German

British soldiers take up positions behind a ridge during the Battle of the Marne in 1914.

armies attempted to pierce Allied defenses. General Alexander von Kluck commanded the German First Army, and General Karl von Bülow the German Second Army.

The French attacked to break up the strong German formations coming at them. They succeeded in turning Kluck's First Army by attacking its right flank. The action opened up a gap between the two German armies, which the Allies rushed troops into. Although the Germans were close to breaking through French lines, the Allied tactics disrupted the German line of advance. When it became clear that Allied troops threatened to surround both German armies, the Germans pulled back. They marched for 40 miles (64km) to the Aisne River, fighting the entire way.

The First Battle of the Marne, which lasted from September 5 to September 12, 1914, was a crucial success for the Allied armies. They had prevented the Germans from reaching Paris and foiled the Schlieffen Plan. Ferdinand Foch, commander of the French Ninth Army at the Battle of the Marne, described the significance in his memoirs:

> Our adversary was dangerously superior to us in the modern war material which he had been preparing for many years and was now using with great effect. In spite of that and of the exceptional nature of the terrain here in Lorraine, his first dash had been checked and he had failed to obtain a decisive result. He had not been able to bring about that rapid and victorious march of

events which his undoubted superiority in men and armaments had led him to expect.[11]

The Race to the Sea

Paris had been saved, but the Germans were by no means beaten. In fact, an extraordinary effort to create defensive positions followed when the Germans stopped along the Aisne River. While some German units entrenched, others attempted to move northward around the Allied armies. The Allies, likewise, moved northward attempting to get around the Germans. Both sides dug trenches in the earth to defend against an attack. The digging of roughly parallel lines northward toward the coast became popularly known as the "race to the sea." But the sea itself was never the objective. The French commander Foch found the term highly deceptive:

> It sounds well but it does not give a true idea of the operations; nor does it really reflect the idea on which these operations were based. The race was towards the enemy. It was his right wing that we attempted to outflank and envelop; when he outstripped us, it was his effort to outflank us that we warded off. For he was trying by increased speed to envelop us in a maneuver similar to our own. This produced on each side a race towards the northern wing of the opposing army. . . . In this way, the sea marked the end of the maneuver, though it had never been its aim.[12]

The trenches ultimately stretched from the coast of Belgium just north of Nieuwpoort south all the way to Switzerland. These lines stayed more or less the same from 1914 to 1918. During the coming years, each side would batter the other and sometimes gain ground. Many of the battles fought over the next four years attempted to remove a bump in the line, known as a salient, which protruded dangerously away from the main line of defense. Millions of men died simply smoothing the line, removing the salients.

Life in the Trench

Trench warfare took on a grim monotony interrupted only by the terror of an attack. Soldiers learned to live in the mud of the trenches, never leaving unless they were taken off the line for rest or moving forward on the attack. Attacks also took on an unreal repetitiveness. First, the artillery would pound enemy positions attempting to break up defenses, knock out guns, and blow holes in barbed wire, used by both sides to hinder men trying to enter their trenches. After the artillery barrages, the men charged forward over the top of their trenches and attacked enemy positions. Enemy machine-gun and rifle fire caused thousands of men to die in single attacks. The machine gun and barbed wire made this a war of defense. Neither army could break the battle line of the other.

Life in the Trenches

Most soldiers on the western front lived like burrowing animals. Their trenches, dug from the earth with small shovels, became home. On sunny days, a sliver of blue overhead was all of the sky they saw. The trenches ran for miles, connecting with each other like roads. Dugouts provided officers with temporary offices and sleeping quarters. The common soldier often slept in a tiny pit dug in the side of the trench.

Soldiers learned to keep their heads down, running hunched over so as not to get hit by a sniper or flying shrapnel from enemy artillery. Many nonetheless were buried alive in bombardments. The rat provided a constant companion for the soldiers. Rats were much hated because they carried disease and fed on the corpses of dead soldiers.

Separating the trenches of the Allied and Central powers was no-man's-land, a stretch of shell-pocked earth where no living thing grew. Unless ordered to attack across no-man's-land, soldiers ventured into the area only at night to check their defenses and spy on the enemy.

Manning trenches across such a long area took millions of soldiers. The British and French turned to their colonies for more manpower, and soon Canadians, Australians, New Zealanders, and soldiers from the British colony of India were fighting alongside the British. Likewise, the French called on troops from their African and Southeast Asian colonies. China also sent laborers to support the troops by moving supplies and providing food and other services.

These new troops fought alongside the forces of the British and French. The

Fighting from fixed positions in filthy trenches, thousands of men died while trying to leave the trenches to advance on enemy positions. Here, a British unit goes "over the top" to engage the German army.

The Hero of Verdun

German troops attempted to pierce Allied defenses along the western front at many places. For the French, perhaps the most famous of all is Verdun, where French troops held their ground during ten months of German attacks. The commander of Verdun, Henri Philippe Pétain, earned the nickname the "savior of Verdun" and was awarded the distinction of Marshal of France, a coveted award given to France's most celebrated generals. For Pétain, World War I left him with fame and glory, but the story does not stop there.

During World War II the Germans conquered all of France. In the southern part of the country, they allowed a new French state to appear—Vichy France. With its capital at the resort town of Vichy, this new state was friendly to the Nazis and allowed them to concentrate their forces elsewhere. The leader of Vichy France was Pétain. Once famous for defending France from Germany, he ruled from 1940 to 1944 as a collaborator of the Nazi occupation of France. After the war he was convicted of treason, though spared the death penalty because of his contributions to the defense of France during World War I.

Canadians, for example, fought valiantly at the Second Battle of Ypres, a city in Belgium, which was fought from late April to late May 1915. The Allied forces attempted to break through the German lines near the city, which was important because it blocked the route into northern France. To break the stalemate of trench warfare and stop the Allied advance, the Germans made use of a sinister new weapon—poison gas. The British general Sir John French recorded its effects when it was used against a section of the line manned by French soldiers on April 22, 1915:

Following a heavy bombardment, the enemy attacked the French Division at about 5 p.m., using asphyxiating gases for the first time. Aircraft reported that at about 5 p.m. thick yellow smoke had been seen issuing from the German trenches. . . . What followed almost defies description. The effect of these poisonous gases was so virulent as to render the whole of the line held by the French Division mentioned above practically incapable of any action at all. . . . The smoke and fumes hid everything from sight, and hundreds of men were thrown into a comatose or dying condition, and within an hour the whole position had to be abandoned.[13]

German soldiers and their dogs man their positions wearing gas masks.

The Germans had signed an agreement prohibiting the use of poison gas shells at the Hague Conference in 1899, but they abandoned the restriction to try to break the stalemate on the western front. The British and French followed suit. But poison gas depended on wind conditions, and it sometimes blew back into the trenches of the army that had released it. Though a terrifying weapon, gas never enabled a breakthrough by one side or the other. It did, however, become a part of life in the trenches.

The gas mask, which protected soldiers from breathing in the gas or being blinded by it, became a regular feature of life in the trenches. It gave the men a strange, alien-like appearance, but trench warfare in fact presented many eerie spectacles. The constant shelling flattened the earth, killed the trees, and drove off animals and birds. Men fought in a desolate landscape that some described as looking like the surface of the moon. During the wet winter months, water flooded the trenches and the shell craters marking the battlefields. Men lived knee-deep in water and mud. Soldiers laid wooden planks known as duckboards across the slippery land, and the war continued.

The Mincing Machine of Verdun

Held in Belgium and northern France, the Germans attempted to pressure the French armies guarding the ancient fortified town of Verdun to the south. The Germans believed they could put sufficient pressure on the French to cause a collapse in morale. The Battle of Verdun, the longest in history, lasted for ten months, from February 21, 1916, to December 18, 1916.

The Germans opened the battle with a barrage of over a million shells fired at the French positions. The French were pushed back by waves of German assault troops, who used flamethrowers to burn the French out of the trenches. To prevent a complete collapse in the area, the French rushed in reinforcements and gave command to General Philippe Pétain to coordinate defenses. More than a quarter of a million men died in the fighting, and Verdun became known as the "mincing machine of Verdun." Although suffering many more casualties than the Germans, the French held, and Pétain was known ever after as the "savior of Verdun." By December 1916, the battlefield resembled once again a lunar landscape, muddy, wet, and miserable. The German assault ground to a halt.

Although millions died on the western front, little changed in the years after both armies dug into their trenches. The war on the western front would remain for the duration the center of the storm, but both the Central Powers and the Allies constantly sought new areas and new strategies to gain the advantage.

Chapter Two

War on the Sea and in the Air

With the armies in Europe mired in their trenches and no clear path to victory, military planners from both sides sought alternative strategies to attack their enemies. International trade during World War I was as important as it is today, and both the Central Powers and the Allies struggled for mastery of the seas, through which much of that trade traveled.

From the outset of hostilities, the seas became a battlefield, and in time a new kind of war appeared in the skies above. World War I gave birth to the modern air force as an independent branch of the military. Its advocates saw in the bomber a way to break the will of defenders on the ground and help strangle, along with the navy, the economy of an enemy.

Challenging the British Royal Navy

The arms race that preceded World War I resulted from the German decision to establish itself as a world-class naval power. Germany, hungry for both overseas colonies and prestige, knew that only a navy could guard the routes to colonies and protect troops sent abroad. Germany also hoped to challenge the might of the British royal navy, the most powerful navy of the time.

The British navy was the envy of Europe. Not only could it defend the island nation, but it also allowed for the British to found a worldwide empire stretching from the British Isles around the globe through Africa, India, China, Australia, New Zealand, and Canada. The navy provided protection for the sea lanes along which colonial commerce sailed. It also made Britain a world military power, able to influence world events. Winston Churchill, who served as the first sea lord, or head of the British navy at the beginning of World War I, summed up the importance of the navy to the British:

The transport ship U.S.S. Covington *sinks after being torpedoed by a German submarine off the coast of France on July 1, 1918.*

Great Britain, deprived of its naval defence, could be speedily starved into utter submission to the will of the conqueror. Her Empire would be dismembered; her dominions, India and her immense African and island possessions would be shorn off or transferred to the victors. . . . The stakes were very high. If our naval defence were maintained we were safe and sure beyond the lot of any other European nation; if it failed our doom was certain and final.[14]

By the early twentieth century other nations had begun to challenge British dominance of the seas. If a nation made use of technological advances and spent adequate money on men and ships, it could build a great navy. The Japanese proved this in 1905. Japan had adopted Western scientific methods to make its navy the equal of Western navies, and when war broke out with Russia, Japan got a chance to put its navy to the test.

To support Russian ground forces fighting the Japanese in northeastern China, Russia sent its Baltic fleet around the globe. The 20,000-mile voyage (32,187km) around Europe, Africa, India, and finally up the coast of China allowed the large Russian fleet to meet the Japanese imperial navy in the Tsushima Strait between Japan and Korea. In the two-day battle that ensued, Japan destroyed the Russian fleet completely.

The rise of Japanese naval power and the growing navy of the United States indicated a new age of naval competition. Of all nations, the British had the most

Ideas for Admirals

Certain books in history have changed the course of world events. One such book was *The Influence of Sea Power Upon History, 1660–1783,* by Alfred Thayer Mahan, published in 1890. After serving in the U.S. Navy, Mahan became a lecturer at the Naval War College and helped shape future U.S. naval leaders. His theories about sea power echoed far beyond.

In his most famous book, Mahan examined the traditional rivalry between Great Britain and France. He argued that Britain ultimately came out ahead and expanded its influence because of the strength of its navies. Mahan believed that the use of technology to improve fighting ships provided the decisive factor in modern naval warfare. His book was read by leaders around the world and studied closely in Britain. In Germany the kaiser also studied the book, which fired his own desire for a great naval fleet for Germany.

to lose, since their defense depended on the navy and because they did not wish to give up their reputation as the world's greatest sea power. Once Germany decided to challenge British power at sea, the British had no choice but to keep ahead of the Germans by building ever bigger and more powerful battleships.

The Dreaded *Dreadnought*

The first of the new battleships was the *Dreadnought*, which gave its name to an entire class of enormous, heavily armed warships. So powerful was the new ship that no other ship on the seas could defeat it in open battle. The Germans responded by building their own dreadnought-class warships. From the British point of view, it was a matter of life or death. Sir Edward Grey, Britain's foreign secretary, made this clear in a statement to Parliament in 1909, calling for more funds to be made available for the building of Britain's own dreadnoughts:

The HMS Dreadnought *was in a new class of "big gun" battleships. Navies throughout the world imitated the design of this ship after its first launch in 1906.*

The German view of their program is that it is made for their own needs, and has no reference to ours, and that if we build fifty or a hundred Dreadnoughts they will not build more, but if we cease building altogether they will not build one less. . . . It is essential to us that we should not fall into a position of inferiority; it is essential that we should keep a position of superiority as regards our navy.[15]

By the outbreak of World War I, Britain had managed to stay ahead in the naval arms race. The British Grand Fleet expected to meet the German High Seas Fleet for a decisive battle at the outset of the war. The winning side, it was supposed, would be able to cut off supplies to the losing side, and thus shorten a ground war. Because the British had the advantage at sea, the Germans hoped to lure the royal navy into attacking German ships at fortified points. The center of the trap was to be Heligoland Bight on the coast of northern Europe. The Germans hoped to use long-range artillery and sea mines to sink British ships while their own ships slipped behind the screen of shore-based gunfire and floating mines.

The Opening Sea Battles

The British Grand Fleet was based at Scapa Flow in the Orkney Islands at the extreme northern tip of Great Britain and at two other Scottish harbors south of Scapa Flow. Geography had left the German fleet only a stretch of the North Sea across from Scotland from which to emerge for battle. Vice Admiral Sir David Beatty laid his own trap for the German navy on August 28, 1914, as his ships approached the Heligoland Bight hoping to catch the German cruisers as they sallied out to protect the larger German battleships.

British ships were already engaging the Germans when Beatty's main fleet arrived. The British sank three German light cruisers and a destroyer, while only suffering serious damage to one of their cruisers. German reinforcements sailed toward the battle, but by the time they arrived, the two forces had lost contact and the battle was at an end. This early sea battle indicated that the British retained their mastery of the seas. Yet the main German High Seas Fleet with its dreadnought-class vessels had not yet been engaged.

During the early years of the war at sea, the British spent much time hunting down German cruisers that sank merchant ships around the globe. This war against commerce was intended to destroy Allied shipping, depriving Great Britain and France of supplies purchased from neutral countries like the United States. The Germans used a combination of their fast cruisers and the dreaded U-boat, or submarine.

Terror from Beneath the Waves

Although the Germans had failed to overtake the British in the dreadnought race, they had advanced sufficiently to unleash a new type of warfare under the water. Because they were small and could travel underwater, German submarines known as U-boats could slip through Allied defenses. They preyed on ships that were generally unaware of their presence. In the

German sailors load a torpedo aboard a U-boat during World War I.

first weeks of the war, German U-boats sank the British warships *Aboukir*, *Cressy*, and *Hogue*. Although these were not of the modern dreadnought class, their loss by an unseen enemy caused horror in Britain and increased caution among the commanders of the British navy.

German U-boats plagued the Allies for the rest of the war. They could pick off warships, but their true use became apparent as the war wore on and the Allies relied increasingly on supplies purchased from the United States. Just as the British attempted to starve Germany by naval blockade, cutting off supplies flowing into German ports, the Germans attempted to sink ships carrying supplies to Great Britain.

At first, the Germans followed the traditional rules of naval war. Upon sighting an unarmed merchant ship, a German U-boat surfaced and allowed the sailors onboard to climb into the life rafts and float away before sinking the vessel. In response to the British navy's blockade of Germany, however, the Germans in early 1915 declared the area around the British Isles to be a war zone, in which they would give no warning to any ship. Unarmed vessels of any nation would be destroyed without warning by the U-boats.

This policy ran the risk of opening hostilities with the United States, which carried on a busy trade by ship with Britain. Yet many in the German high command did not fear war with the United States. "I look upon a declaration of war by the United States with indifference!"[16] General Erich Ludendorff remarked.

In 1915 the German ambassador announced that the Germans intended to sink the *Lusitania*, a British passenger liner that sailed the transatlantic route. A U-boat sank the ship on May 7, 1915, killing many people including 100 Americans. By sinking the unarmed vessel, the Germans sparked an outcry in the United States to declare war on Germany. Although the U.S. Army was undermanned and ill prepared for war, the U.S. Navy was one of the great navies of the world. President Woodrow Wilson, however, kept the United States out of the war, while protesting to Germany. The German kaiser was not as indifferent as some of his military advisers about war with the United States. And U.S. protests over the sinking of the *Lusitania* caused the kaiser to halt the unrestricted submarine warfare for the time being so as to avoid war with the United States. Nonetheless, Germany needed

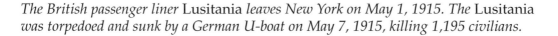

The British passenger liner Lusitania *leaves New York on May 1, 1915. The* Lusitania *was torpedoed and sunk by a German U-boat on May 7, 1915, killing 1,195 civilians.*

The Battle of Lake Tanganyika

When the naval battles of World War I commenced, war broke out in some very remote places. These were the colonies of the European powers, and no naval battle was more unlike the clash of the German High Seas Fleet and the British Grand Fleet than the battle on Lake Tanganyika.

The lake lay at the heart of British and German East Africa, where both powers had colonies. The Europeans in those areas relied on shipping to get supplies and remain in contact with Europe. Both powers wanted to control the waters in the area. At Lake Tanganyika, the Germans armed steamers with guns and patrol the area. To destroy them, the British sent two 40-foot wooden boats—named *Mimi* and *Toutou*—in pieces over land. It was an improbable expedition with many difficulties. Once the boats were assembled, however, they proved their worth, sinking the German steamers and winning the lake for the Allies. The tale is told in detail in Mimi *and* Toutou's *Big Adventure: The Bizarre Battle of Lake Tanganyika* by Giles Foden.

some way to strangle Britain before the British blockade dried up their own supplies.

The Battle of Jutland

In 1916 the Germans provoked a sea battle that would prove to be the largest of World War I. They hoped once again to lure the British fleet into the area west of Jutland, Denmark. The German High Seas Fleet under Admiral Reinhard Scheer hoped to break the blockade that was pressing on the German economy and limiting the effectiveness of the German fleet. He dispatched Vice Admiral Franz von Hipper's task force of five battle cruisers to make contact with the British navy and lure ships into range of the main German force.

The British Admiralty had a distinct advantage before the battle began. Not only was the British fleet larger and more powerful than that of Germany, but the British had gotten hold of German codebooks and could read German naval signals. The communications intelligence allowed the British to fight with a general idea of the German plan.

To intercept the German warships, the British sent a battle cruiser squadron under the command of Vice Admiral Sir David Beatty from the Firth of Forth in Scotland, while the British Grand Fleet of superdreadnoughts—more powerful versions of the already giant warships—steamed from Scapa Flow under the command of Admiral Sir John Jellicoe. The two pincers, or arms of the attack, were to cross the North Sea and close in on the German High Seas Fleet.

Beatty's battle cruisers came into contact with Hipper's squadron on May 31, 1916, and the Battle of Jutland ensued. It was the greatest naval battle of the war and the last great naval battle fought without airplanes supporting the warships. The fast-moving cruiser squadrons were armed with long-range guns, and both fired with considerable accuracy, sending giant explosions rocketing upward from ships struck by their salvos. The British quickly lost the battle cruisers *Indefatigable* and the *Queen Mary*, and Beatty's own ship, the *Lion*, was on fire, leading him to exclaim, "There seems to be something wrong with our bloody ships today."[17]

After these initial German successes, Hipper turned southward to draw Beatty into the waiting guns of the High Seas Fleet. Upon sighting the fleet, however, Beatty reversed course and drew the Germans toward the north and Jellicoe's main battle force. When the two fleets met, the Germans received a withering bombardment from the British. Confusion and the growing darkness of evening caused the two fleets to make critical errors of judgment. Although many German ships were sunk, the main fleet slipped back once more toward safe harbors in Germany. The British, with the more powerful armada, had failed to destroy the High Seas Fleet.

The Battle of Jutland was thus inconclusive. Neither fleet succeeded in winning a decisive victory over the other. The German fleet never again engaged the more powerful British in open naval warfare. Instead, the war at sea came to resemble a nautical hunt. The Germans hunted Allied shipping with their U-boats, and the Allies hunted the U-boats and German cruisers still loose on the seas. The war at sea after the Battle of Jutland took on the cautiousness of troops on the western front. A decisive breakthrough could not be won. Submarines and sea mines used by both sides made it highly dangerous for warships to sail in contested waters. The war at sea turned to a war of attrition—trying to starve the enemy of supplies from seagoing shipping. The U-boat and the mine, like the mortar and machine gun on the western front, favored the defenders and prevented decisive attacks. Winston Churchill described the frustrating situation in his postwar writings:

Mechanical not less than strategic conditions had combined to produce at this early period in the war a deadlock both on sea and land. The strongest fleet was paralysed in its offensive by the menace of the mine and the torpedo. The strongest army was arrested in its advance by the machine gun. On getting into certain positions necessary for offensive action, ships were sunk by under-water explosions, and soldiers were cut down by streams of bullets. This was the evil which lay at the root of all our perplexities. It was no use endeavouring to remedy this evil on sea by keeping the ships in harbour, or on

The British battle cruiser Queen Mary *explodes after being hit during the Battle of Jutland in 1916. The largest naval battle of the war, it was also the last naval battle fought without the advantage of airplanes protecting the ships from the air.*

land by squandering the lives and valour of endless masses of men. The mechanical danger must be overcome by a mechanical remedy.[18]

Weapons Above

One of the most promising of mechanical remedies to the problems presented both by the deadlock on land and the war at sea was the use of aircraft for military purposes. Troops hunched in the trenches could not see the enemy, just as warships had to hunt each other over vast stretches of water. The possibility of using aircraft to find the enemy spurred both sides rapidly to develop aircraft technology.

To observe the enemy, both sides made use of manned floating balloons and airplanes. Balloons were considerably more difficult to navigate and had to drift over enemy positions. The Germans thus used floating craft that could be piloted. This was the dirigible, a giant floating blimp propelled by an engine. Known as zeppelins, these blimps carried passengers in peacetime. In war, they could photograph enemy positions and drop bombs.

The Birth of Aerial Bombing

Although many military planners were skeptical of the use of airplanes and blimps, being attacked by air presented a terrifying and demoralizing kind of war. When zeppelins first dropped incendiary bombs on England in 1915, a new type of war had dawned. Although the bomb damage was minimal, civilians died, and political leaders feared the effects on the

The Germans used zeppelins in aerial bombing raids.

populace. Suddenly, protecting the coast of the British Isles was not enough. Attackers could arrive overhead in the dead of night, detected only when their bombs began hitting the ground and exploding into fiery fragments.

The zeppelin raids sparked the quick development of ground defenses against air attack. The government required citizens to black out their windows at night to deprive the aerial attackers of targets. The British also trained spotlights on the sky to find the airships before they dropped their bombs. Once spotted, they unleashed fire from specially designed antiaircraft guns that dispersed exploding shells to hit a wide area in the sky.

The size of the zeppelin allowed it to carry a large bomb load, but it also made it an easy target. Many zeppelins were shot down in the war, and their role as spotters better served the Germans.

Throughout the war, zeppelins floated over the Baltic and the North Sea watching for the approach of enemy warships.

Airships proved especially easy prey to aerial defenders. When the war began, none of the combatants had an air force. Armies made use of planes as spotters and sometimes dropped bombs from them by hand, but these caused little damage. By the end of the war, the skies over Europe began to fill with airplanes armed with machine guns and mechanical bomb-dropping devices.

Knights of the Air

The French excelled at building light fighters out of wood harvested in France. Their air force grew rapidly during World War I. These planes were light and easy to fly. They were also very slow, making them easy to bring down by ground fire. Planes became a regular feature above the

The Red Baron

Pilots in World War I dueled one-on-one much like knights had dueled on horseback in the Middle Ages. The air war thus introduced a new figure in military mythology—the flying ace. Because the pilots named their planes and designed their own insignia, they took on the aura of individual warriors, so unlike the millions of men huddled anonymously in the mud of the trenches. Aces competed with each other to down the most enemy airplanes, and their exploits caught the imagination of civilians back at home.

The most successful fighter ace of World War I was the German pilot Manfred von Richthofen, known to history as the Red Baron. Between September 1916 and his death in April 1918, Richthofen shot down eighty enemy planes. He became the terror of the western front and the most feared pilot in the war. In one month alone, April 1917, he

downed twenty-two British aircraft. He flew a number of planes during his career but became associated with his last plane, a single-seat Fokker Dr. I, which had a stack of three wings. One of his planes was painted red, giving rise to his nickname. On April 21, 1918, Richthofen met the fate he had delivered to so many other pilots. He was shot down over France, but not by another pilot. The bullet that killed him came from a soldier on the ground.

Baron Manfred von Richthofen, the "Red Baron."

The Handley Page V1500 bomber saw action on the western front and in the deserts of the Middle East during the war.

trenches, and many pilots perished while flying over enemy territory.

To counter Allied aircraft, the Germans developed a Fokker fighter, named after its Dutch inventor. The plane had a propeller timed with the machine gun so that a pilot could fire to the front at another plane while he was maneuvering his own plane. The Allies quickly copied the technology, and their own pilots dueled with German pilots in single combat in the air. Both sides produced airplanes faster than they could be shot down, and the air forces grew to a considerable size but failed to win the skies for either side.

Perhaps the most promising of all the uses of the airplane during World War I was as a bomber. Larger planes such as the British Handley Page held in their bellies large bombs much like the zeppelins. The Handley Page, which first saw action on the western front in 1917, was used to bomb railways that moved German troops to the front. By the end of the war, this bomber served in the deserts of the Middle East as well, terrifying Turkish troops exposed in the open below.

By the end of the war, the British added to its armed forces the Royal Air Force, a distinct branch devoted exclusively to airpower. Ever after, war would be fought with air support, but the time had not yet come. Although both the Allies and the Central Powers made fantastic technical progress in producing all kinds of aircraft, the air war, like the war at sea, failed to change the course of the war. Airplanes would one day make trench warfare impractical, but the air force was still in its infancy in World War I. Soldiers on the ground would have to keep slogging it out, even as war leaders planned for new offensives to break the deadlock.

Chapter Three

War in the Near East

With the failure of the German and British fleets to settle the war at sea and with the air war unable to make a decisive breakthrough on the western front, the Allied Powers attempted to break the European deadlock by opening new fronts against Turkey.

From the early days of the war, debate among the Allies split between two camps, known as the Westerners and the Easterners. The Westerners argued that Allied resources should not be diverted to new campaigns until the war on the western front was won. They argued that any diversion of men and war matériel from France and Belgium would only drag out the war against the Germans.

The Easterners argued that with the troops pinned down in the trenches, attacks elsewhere could take the pressure off the troops in Europe and help sap the strength of the Central Powers. What the Easterners spoke of was not the eastern front, on which the Russians battled the forces of Germany and Austria-Hungary, but of new fronts away from the main European battlefields.

Undermining the Ottoman Empire

Allied strategists believed that the Ottoman Empire, as the weakest of the Central Powers, should be the target of the new campaign. The Ottoman Empire had been founded in the last year of the thirteenth century and had expanded from its capital at Constantinople (present-day Istanbul in Turkey) into southern Europe, through the Middle East and across North Africa, and down the eastern coast of Africa to the horn.

By October 1914, when the Turks joined the Central Powers, the Ottoman Empire was wobbly. Peoples throughout the empire advocated an end to Ottoman rule, from the Balkans in Europe to the desert tribes of the Arabian Peninsula. Some parts of the empire had in fact already fallen away from the rulers at Constantinople. The Austro-Hungarian Empire had taken some Balkan lands once ruled by the Turks, and Egypt, still nominally part of the Ottoman Empire, was in fact ruled by the British.

The Allied war against the Turks falls into three distinct campaigns. The first was to be one of the greatest Allied disasters of the war—the attempt to capture Constantinople by landing troops on the Gallipoli Peninsula and sailing warships through the narrow Dardanelles, a seaway that leads to Constantinople. After the Gallipoli campaign, the Allies attacked the Turks first in Mesopotamia (present-day Iraq) and then in Palestine.

Assault at Gallipoli

The first phase of the war against the Turks, the Gallipoli campaign, found an energetic champion in the person of Winston Churchill. As first lord of the admiralty, the civilian chief of Britain's naval forces, Churchill submitted a plan to attack Turkey by sea. With his characteristic sense of adventure and daring, Churchill's plan intended to capture Constantinople directly, thus knocking Turkey out of the war with a single fell swoop. "I wanted Gallipoli attacked on the declaration of war,"[19] he wrote in his own history of the First World War.

An opportunity to put the plan into action arrived in 1915 when the secretary of state for war, Lord Kitchener, asked his naval chief, "Do you think any naval action would be possible to prevent [the] Turks sending more men into the Caucasus and thus denuding Constantino-ple?"[20] The British had received a plea from the Russians to take pressure off Russian troops fighting Turkish troops in the Caucasus, a region between the Black and Caspian seas.

Churchill scraped together an armada of warships too obsolete to throw against the German High Seas Fleet. The original plan called only for a naval action, but Kitchener authorized a landing force made up of British units and soldiers from Australia and New Zealand who had recently arrived in Egypt on their way to the western front. The French also contributed troops, including soldiers from their African colony Senegal. This international force was to land on the southern tip and western coast of the Gallipoli Peninsula and cut westward through Turkish defenses to capture the coastal guns guarding the narrow point of the Dardanelles. The royal navy would then sail northward until it reached Constantinople, the capital of the Ottoman Empire.

While the army mobilized and sailed toward Turkey, British and French warships attacked the twin coasts of the Dardanelles beginning on February 19, 1915. The warships' guns pounded Turkish shore positions, and raiding parties were landed to blow up forts and gun emplacements. This was exactly the naval operation that Churchill had imagined. And at the outset, the armada appeared to menace the Turks at will, since the Ottoman Empire had no navy to meet the Allied assault. The Turks did, however, have a weapon fearsome to Allied warships—the floating sea mine.

A naval airship takes to the air in the Dardanelles near Turkey. Many of these airships were used for aerial observation during the battle at Gallipoli in 1915.

Foiled at Sea

Tiny minesweepers attempted to clear a path for the Allied ships, but as the naval force moved closer into the Dardanelles—toward the narrowest and most dangerous point—the Turks were able to unleash fierce barrages from guns on the shore. This prevented the minesweepers from doing their work, and disaster for the British fleet followed. In quick succession, the Allies

The Lone Diversion

The Dardanelles, the narrow waterway that connects the Sea of Marmara and the Aegean Sea, has seen its share of heroes in history and in myth. The ancient city of Troy was located nearby and provided the setting for the Trojan Wars, the subject of Homer's *Iliad*. As a natural passageway between Europe and Asia, the waterway was also crossed by the armies of Alexander the Great, the ancient Greek hero, and the armies of Xerxes, the king of the Persians.

In World War I, a particularly eccentric hero added his own daring exploits to the history of the region. His name was Lieutenant General Bernard Cyril Freyberg, 1st Baron Freyberg. Born in England, Freyberg grew up in New Zealand, where he was an ardent swimmer and later began a profession as a dentist before earning a reputation for daring as a soldier. After volunteering for the Gallipoli campaign, Freyberg jumped ship on the western side of the Gallipoli Peninsula and swam to shore north of the Allied landings. Freyberg single-handedly distracted Turkish units by lighting fires along the coast to trick them into thinking he himself was the invasion force. He later made it safely back to the Allied lines and served on the western front. He was wounded repeatedly at Gallipoli and in Europe. He finally died of one of his old war wounds, but not until 1963 at the age of seventy-four.

lost two British battleships, the *Ocean* and *Irresistible*, and the French battleship *Bouvet*. A number of other ships also struck mines and limped out of the battle area toward safe harbors. For the Turks it was an enormous boost to morale, and they settled in to counter any further attack at Gallipoli.

In April the invasion force under the command of the British general Sir Ian Hamilton began to disembark on the long, fingerlike Gallipoli Peninsula. British journalist Ellis Ashmead-Bartlett watched as soldiers from the Australian and New Zealand Army Corps, known as ANZACs, landed under fire on April 25:

In the early part of the day heavy casualties were suffered in the boats conveying troops from the destroyers, tugs, and transports. The enemy's sharpshooters, hidden everywhere, concentrated their fire on the boats. When close in, at least three boats broke away from their tow and drifted down the coast without control, being sniped at the whole way, and steadily losing men.

The work of disembarking proceeded mechanically under a point-blank fire. The moment the boats touched the beach the troops jumped ashore and doubled for cover; but the gallant boat crews had to pull in and out under a galling fire from hundreds of points.[21]

Despite the heavy fire from the hills overlooking the landing beaches, the Allies successfully gained a foothold on the peninsula and began to move toward higher ground even as supplies and reinforcements followed from the naval armada. The feeling was one of relief and elation, for just across the peninsula lay the Dardanelles and the coast of Asia.

"The purple hills of Asia fade from view," wrote Geoffrey Dearmer, an English soldier who landed with the invasion force, "And rolling battleships at anchor ride."[22]

The Allied objective was to cross the peninsula and capture the shore positions on the other side facing the Dardanelles, thus opening the route for the navy. But between the two sides of the Gallipoli Peninsula stretched rocky highlands and entrenched Turkish positions. The defenders were led by Liman von Sanders, a German of considerable ability, who

British and French troops prepare to battle Turkish forces at the Gallipoli Peninsula in 1915.

managed the front admirably. Once the Allied forces landed, he rushed reinforcements into place on the heights.

The ANZACs attempted to climb the heights and route the Turks in the nighttime. They came very close to succeeding but suffered heavy losses. In the end, they faced Turkey's most determined troop commander, Mustafa Kemal, who scrambled from place to place reassuring his troops and directing fire. The daring nighttime expedition failed, and both sides settled into trenches.

"The Terrible 'Ifs' Accumulate"

Life on Gallipoli quickly began to resemble life on the western front. Men crouched in trenches and suffered bitterly from machine-gun and rifle fire when they attacked the enemy positions. Be-

cause of the perceived corruption and inefficiency of the Ottoman Empire, Turkey had been called the "sick man of Europe" by the Russians before the war. But Allied soldiers gained a new respect for the Turks as fighting men. "On the defensive," wrote one British commander, "his eye for ground, his skill in planning and entrenching a position, and his stubbornness in holding it made him a really formidable adversary to engage."[23]

Winston Churchill, the campaign's greatest supporter, watched as one thing after another went wrong: "The terrible 'ifs' accumulate,"[24] he said. If only the navy had not run into the mines, if only the soldiers had forced their way over the ridges, the campaign might have worked—but in the end it failed. By winter, the Allies plucked their troops off the peninsula and sailed away. Constantinople was safe.

Members of the Australian and New Zealand Army Corps, known as ANZACs, rest at their camp position during the battle of Gallipoli.

Father of the Turks

Oone soldier in particular who fought on Gallipoli was destined to shape the course of modern history. He was the commander of the Nineteenth Division of the Turkish Fifth Army. His name was Mustafa Kemal, but he would earn worldwide fame and the affection of the Turkish people under the name Atatürk, which translates as "father of the Turks."

After successfully leading his troops in the defense of Gallipoli and attempting to repel the British advance under General Allenby in Palestine, Atatürk became disillusioned with the Ottoman leaders in Constantinople. He dreamed of reviving Turkey as a modern state, ridding it of leaders he thought were out of touch with the modern world. After Turkey's defeat in World War I, Atatürk set up a rival capital in Ankara, raised an army, drove the Allied occupation forces out of Turkey, and founded the modern state of Turkey. He abandoned all claims to the Ottoman territories of old, separated religion and politics, and instituted a host of reforms that allowed Turkey to rise up as a proud new nation.

Mustafa Kemal Atatürk.

Churchill bore the responsibility and lost his post as first sea lord. For Australia and New Zealand, whose troops were mostly fresh recruits, Gallipoli left a bitter taste, but it won their soldiers a reputation for heroic bravery.

After the failure to knock Turkey out of the war by a direct attack on Turkish soil, the Allies attempted to roll up the Ottoman Empire from its outer ends, attacking instead through distant Ottoman provinces. The first of the two other major campaigns against the Ottoman Empire attempted to slice northward through Mesopotamia, present-day Iraq.

The British Indian Army in Iraq

So as not to weaken forces on the western front, the Mesopotamian campaign fell to the Indian army. India, the largest of the British colonies, was a fairly self-sufficient enterprise. It was ruled by a British viceroy, who took orders from London but often acted with a great deal of independence. To guard the colony, the British in India raised an army from the various races and religions of the subcontinent. The regimental system in some ways mirrored that of the British home armies. Regiments recruited independently. Muslims often fought in Muslim regiments, Sikhs in Sikh regiments, and so on. All of these regiments were commanded by British officers. Indians were allowed to move up in the ranks slowly, though never to the highest posts.

At the outset of hostilities with Turkey, the British had landed an Indian army force in the Persian Gulf, which set up camp near the Shatt al Arab, a river formed by the joining of the Tigris and Euphrates, Iraq's two main rivers. The Shatt al Arab spills into the Persian Gulf and forms the border between Iraq and Iran. It has a low-lying delta and provides a good landing spot for sea traffic.

From this base, the British marched up the river and captured Basra, a major city in southern Mesopotamia, from the Turks. British interest in the region largely focused on securing the oil fields of the Anglo-Persian Oil Company. After Gallipoli, however, the expeditionary force hoped to restore British prestige by capturing Baghdad. Capturing this ancient city from the Turks was not a military necessity, but it was believed it would boost morale of the British at home.

An advance up the Tigris was authorized by the British viceroy in India, and Major General Sir Charles Townshend led the expedition. He was an eccentric officer, not popular with his men, and constantly accompanied by his dog, Spot. The British force marched in August 1915, in the relentless heat and across a parched landscape. Townshend's force clashed with the Turks along the route and by late September captured the town of Al Kūt, about 100 miles (161km) south of Baghdad.

The Siege at Al Kūt

The success of the campaign tempted the British to strike northward at Baghdad. The Turks, however, had been regrouping and prepared to stop Townshend's march. The Turks under the command of a German officer, Baron von der Goltz, engaged the British at the city of Ctesiphon, about 20 miles (32km) south of Baghdad. The British were not only outnumbered, but they faced a force dug into well-prepared trenches. Just as at Gallipoli, the Turks proved themselves fierce opponents on the defensive. The British were driven back, pursued by the Turkish forces.

General Townshend retreated until he reached Al Kūt once again, and he de-cided to stay put and wait for a relief force from the south. On December 7, 1915, the Turks arrived and besieged the town, cutting off all escape routes. Although the British forces beat off attacks by the Turks, they were trapped in the small town, growing short of food and losing men from disease and hunger. The siege lasted for 147 days, making it the longest in British military history.

Relief expeditions had been stopped by the Turks, and the entire British army

A U.S. marine clears the area around the Al Kūt War Cemetery outside Baghdad in 2003. In 1915, after a siege of 147 days, the entire British army at Al Kūt was forced to surrender to the Turkish army.

at Al Kūt surrendered. Townshend attempted to bribe the Turks into letting the force withdraw, but they refused. "My duty seems clear," Townshend wrote, "to go into captivity with my force though I know the hot weather will kill me, for the continuous strain I have suffered from August till now is more than I can bear."[25]

Townshend did not die as he predicted. He was treated well by the Turks, who gave him a villa near Constantinople, sent his dog back to England, and later released the general unharmed. His troops, on the other hand, suffered a brutal march from Al Kūt to Turkey, many of them dying along the way from heat, starvation, and disease.

The surrender of the British forces at Al Kūt proved to be a national disgrace and shocked British citizens at home. It added to the failure at Gallipoli another humiliation for the Allied armies, and Turkish pride soared. Allied forces had now been beaten twice by the "sick man of Europe." They began to fear that the Turks would continue their successful campaign right into Egypt.

Defending the Suez Canal

Egypt had a special importance for the British Empire. The Suez Canal, which connected the Mediterranean with the Red Sea, acted as a lifeline for the empire. Ships sailing from Britain to India avoided the long trip around Africa by passing through this man-made canal, and it was vital for the British to protect it at all costs. "The original object of our maintaining a force in Egypt at all was

Turkish soldiers march through the streets of Constantinople (now Istanbul) ready to defend the country from Allied forces during World War I.

quite simple and definite," wrote Archibald Wavell, a British commander in Egypt. "Its role was that of a detachment guarding a vital main line of communication."[26]

The Turks had first advanced to the Suez Canal in early February 1915 in the midst of a blistering sandstorm. The approach from Syria, an Ottoman province at the time, was unopposed until the troops reached the canal after crossing the Sinai Peninsula. Once they reached it, however, they faced a stronger British force and Allied warships, which could direct their guns at shore positions, in the lakes of the canal. The few Turks who made it across the canal were swiftly eliminated by the British, and the Turkish force retreated into the Sinai from which it had come.

The Suez Canal would have been a prize akin to capturing Constantinople for the Allies. For the Turks, however, it was just as much of a dangerous gamble, and it too failed. Because of the threat to the canal, the British sent troops from home to Egypt, even as soldiers from the Gallipoli campaign arrived in the area. The result was a buildup of Allied forces no longer facing a Turkish attack. The British therefore decided to launch another attack against Turkish-controlled territory. They organized the soldiers in Egypt into the Egyptian Expeditionary Force first under the command of General Archibald Murray.

Murray led this army into the Sinai, a peninsula separating Egypt from Arabia. It was an antique land, empty and inhospitable. The peninsula, however, provided a land route to the eastern Mediterranean lands of ancient Palestine (present-day Israel and the Palestinian territories). Murray had decided that the best way to prevent a Turkish attack on the canal was to move out into the Sinai and stop the Turks from this approach. Thus, the strategy to defend the canal turned into an Allied advance directly into Turkish territory.

Allied Troops on the Offensive

By the end of 1916 Murray's forces had driven the Turks out of the Sinai and encamped in defensive positions across the border of Palestine. At this point, the debate between Easterners and Westerners once again heated up. Murray's orders had been to defend the canal, but his success prompted the Easterners to advocate a further advance. The Westerners once again argued that this would take troops away from the main war in Europe. They dubbed the Middle East campaign a "side show." Archibald Wavell, a British officer who fought the Turks in the Middle East, strongly disagreed. "The campaigns of the Egyptian Expeditionary Force have been frequently termed a 'side show,'" he wrote. "If this expression is intended to imply that the campaigns were planned and executed independently of the march of events in the main theatre of war in Europe or in the other theatres, it is certainly misapplied."[27]

Although waging war in the Middle East might tie up troops that could be sent to Europe, it also tied up Turkish

The Making of a Legend

In 1917, after the United States declared war on Germany, a group of businesspeople in Chicago hired Lowell Thomas, a newspaper reporter, to travel to the western front and find stories to popularize the war at home. He found the war on the western front so grim that he eventually turned to the Middle East campaign, where he found a young British officer aiding a revolt by the Arabs against Ottoman Turkish rule.

The Arab revolt was everything that the western front was not. The soldiers fought on horseback in the open desert, much as they had done for centuries. The British officer, Thomas Edward Lawrence, moreover, looked nothing like the mud-covered, green-uniformed soldiers stuck in the trenches in Europe. He wore white Arab robes and a traditional Arab headdress and fought on the back of a camel. Thomas had found his story. He publicized it through a series of dramatically colored slide shows in the United States and Britain, giving birth to the legend of Lawrence of Arabia, one of the most colorful heroes to emerge from the First World War.

troops who would otherwise be free to fight the Russians. Moreover, the success of the Egyptian Expeditionary Force helped to restore confidence and undo the damage done to Britain's prestige in Gallipoli and Mesopotamia.

From the Allied point of view, there was another reason to keep the Turks on the defensive in the Middle East. As part of their strategy to stir up a revolt against the British in Egypt and India, the Germans and Turks attempted to start a holy war of Muslims against non-Muslim occupiers. Egypt was overwhelmingly Muslim, and India had many Muslims serving in the Indian army. The Allies believed that by capturing from the Turks the Muslim holy cities of Mecca and Medina along the coast of Arabia in an area known as the Hejaz, they could prevent an Islamic revolt from brewing.

The Arab Revolt

To capture these sacred cities, the British sent officers to organize Arab forces already clashing with their Turkish rulers in Arabia. Thomas Edward Lawrence, one of these British officers, found among the Arabian leaders one whom he thought could successfully lead the revolt. This was Prince Faisal, whose family was revered because of their ancestral connection to the Prophet Muhammad. "I felt at first glance that this was the man I had come to Arabia to seek—the leader who would bring the Arab Revolt to full glory,"[28] wrote Lawrence.

Faisal's father was considered the rightful protector of the holy cities, and was held therefore as a well-treated prisoner of the Turks in Constantinople. Faisal, however, with his brothers had decided that Arabia would be better off without the Turks, and he provided a figurehead for the Arab Revolt. Faisal's leadership gave the revolt against the Turks a legitimacy it would otherwise not have had. Moreover, as a revered Muslim leader and guardian of the holy cities, he countered the attempt of the Central Powers to create a religious war. The Arabs, wrote Lawrence,

knew that the British were Christians, and that the British were their allies. In the circumstances, their religion would not have been of much help to them, and they had put it aside. "Christian fights Christian, so why should not Mohammedans [Muslims] do the same? What we want is a Government which speaks our own language of Arabic and will let us live in peace. Also we hate those Turks."[29]

Ancient Ways of War

The Arab Revolt more resembled ancient warfare than the modern mechanized war in Europe. Arab soldiers fought on horse and camelback, raiding Turkish positions along a railway that ran along the eastern coast of the Arabian Peninsula.

The goal of the Arab army was in fact not to defeat the Turks and drive them out of Arabia, but to pin them down along the railway so that troops would be bottled up and unable to advance or retreat. Medina, which was garrisoned by Turkish troops, was the main object of this tactic. "Making the maintenance of the Turkish garrison at Medina just a shade

T.E. Lawrence was charged with finding Arab allies who would help the British by leading a revolt against the Turkish rulers in Arabia.

less difficult than its evacuation would serve the interests of British and Arab alike,"[30] Lawrence wrote.

The Arab army then busied itself with blowing up train tracks and making life difficult for the Turks all along the railway. The Arab army was never strong enough to face the Turks head on, and they waged classic guerrilla war. "The death of a Turkish bridge or rail, machine or gun or charge of high explosive," wrote Lawrence, "was more profitable to us than the death of a Turk."[31]

The Capture of Aqaba

There was one spot along the eastern coast of Arabia, however, that provided an important objective for the Allied campaign in Palestine. This was the port city of Aqaba (in present-day Jordan), where the Turks had large shore batteries that could prevent Allied ships from sailing in the area. The Arab army hit upon a daring plan to capture the city by an attack from land. To reach Aqaba, the Arabs marched northward and then took a detour through a blistering desert stretch. They gathered soldiers along the way from the various Arab tribes of the area. The Arabs rode out of the empty land behind Aqaba on July 6, 1917, and captured the Turkish guns, which were fixed toward the sea. The city was caught entirely by surprise, and the Arabs quickly overran the Turkish garrison.

It was a stunning success, and it freed the British to land supplies for the Egyptian Expeditionary Force at the port. After the city fell, Lawrence, who rode with the Arab forces, crossed the Sinai and re-ported the success directly to General Edmund Allenby, who had replaced Murray as commander in the region. "Our capture of Akaba [Aqaba] closed the Hejaz war, and gave us the task of helping the British invade Syria," Lawrence wrote. "The Arabs working from Akaba became the virtual right wing of Allenby's army in Sinai."[32]

Allenby's Push Through Palestine

In fact, at this point the Arab army came under the direct command of Allenby, acting as his right flank in the Palestine campaign. Allenby was then free to advance through Palestine toward the biblical city of Jerusalem. This represented a real threat to Turkish control in the Middle East and the ultimate battle of the campaign against the Turks. In October Allenby forced his way into the Judean Hills, which blocked the path to Jerusalem. Ottoman forces, advised by the German commander General Erich von Falkenhayn, resisted fiercely but could not hold out against the Allied advance. Allenby entered Jerusalem on December 9, 1917.

The city itself, although famous because of its religious significance to Christians, Muslims, and Jews, was not important militarily. Yet the Allied advance into Palestine had driven the Turks back on the defensive in Syria, relieved pressure on British forces in Mesopotamia, and secured once and for all the safety of the Suez Canal. Wavell wrote:

All danger to Baghdad and to the British conquest of Iraq was defi-

General Edmund Allenby arrives in Jerusalem on December 9, 1917.

nitely and finally removed; practically the last Turkish reserves of man power were drawn in; and the British nation received the Christmas present that the Prime Minister had desired for it. Though the occupation of Jerusalem itself had no special strategical importance, its moral significance was great.[33]

Indeed, the British had finally avenged the defeats of Gallipoli and Al Kūt. The British subsequently moved on to Damascus, Syria, with the Arab armies riding on their right. It was a triumph at last for the Easterners. Turkey, now fearing an invasion, was forced on to the defensive, and the other Central Powers were left to fight with a weakened Turkish ally.

War in the Near East ■ 53

Chapter Four

War on the Eastern Front—the Old World Crumbles

The kaiser's abandonment of Germany's cautious policy under Bismarck indicated the confidence of the Germans to fight a two-front war. Showing great contempt for the fighting ability of Russia, the Germans intended at the outset of the war to fight a holding action against the Russians while the Schlieffen Plan quickly defeated France. Although the German battle plan in western Europe failed, Germany's campaign against Russia was the kaiser's most successful of World War I. German success on the battlefield achieved a startling political collapse in Russia, removing the large armies of Russia from the Allied cause and freeing German troops to fight on the western front.

Fighting on the eastern front, the battlefield that stretched north-south from the Baltic to the Black Sea, proved to be considerably different from the fighting on the western front. The battle area was twice as long as the western front. Armies could thus maneuver as they had in past wars. Although trenches were dug on the front, the battle moved quickly, making them obsolete.

A War of Maneuver

When the Germans invaded France in 1914, the Russians, allied to the British and French, launched their own offensive against the Central Powers from the east. The Russian assault came from two directions. In the north, two Russian armies under the command of Paul Rennenkampf and Alexander Samsonov attempted to capture East Prussia by a pincer movement. Victory in East Prussia, a province of imperial Germany along the Baltic Sea, would open a northern corridor directly into the heart of Germany.

Rennenkampf led the northern thrust into East Prussia, while Samsonov's army swung south and then west in an attempt to encircle the German defenders. Rennenkampf was largely successful, driving

Dug in for a Russian attack, German soldiers man a trench line at the Russian eastern front in 1916.

War on the Eastern Front—the Old World Crumbles ■ 55

the Germans back and forcing the kaiser to rush troops from the western front to stop the Russian advance. The German commander panicked, and he was replaced with Paul von Hindenburg in command of the German Eighth Army. With great vigor and intelligence, Hindenburg restored German morale and launched a counteroffensive.

The Battle of Tannenberg

After the initial success of the Russian attack, the two Russian armies paused. German military intelligence had been reading Russian communications and knew that the two Russian armies operated independently. In fact, Rennenkampf had paused to regroup, and the Germans turned on Samsonov's army to the south. The Germans and Russians clashed around the ancient village of Tannenberg on land that today lies in Poland. On encountering the Germans, Samsonov threw his forces forward. Before he realized what had happened, he had been encircled by the Germans, who intentionally drew the Russian forces forward while they moved around the flanks.

When Rennenkampf heard the news from the Battle of Tannenberg, he moved south to assist Samsonov. But it was too late. The Russian Second Army had ceased to exist. The Germans captured about ninety-two thousand Russian soldiers. Only ten thousand managed to slip through the German net. Samsonov shot himself instead of returning to Russia in disgrace.

The Battle of Tannenberg tipped the balance in favor of the Germans on the northern section of the eastern front. The Russians fared better on the southern section of the front. The Russians launched the

Germans man a trench at Tannenberg. At the end of this campaign, the Germans captured about 92,000 Russian soldiers, resulting in a decisive German victory.

The Game Is Afoot

Russia during World War I bubbled with secret plots and conspiracies. While the war continued in the open, a political war was conducted in secret. Bolsheviks and revolutionaries of all stripes plotted to overthrow the czar, while the Russian secret police, the Okhrana, hunted the conspirators. After the Bolsheviks came to power, White Russians, opposed to the Communist government, plotted to retake power.

Both the Central and Allied powers took part in the game, attempting to influence Russian politics with money, information, and disinformation. The Germans sent Bolshevik leader Vladimir Lenin back to Russia in a sealed train across the eastern front to help fell the czar's regime. When Lenin became leader of the Bolshevik government, the Allies hatched a plot to assassinate him. Robert Bruce Lockhart, the British diplomatic representative to both the czarist and Bolshevik governments, was implicated along with Sidney Reilly, a spy working for the British, in a plot to assassinate Lenin. He was imprisoned by the Russians but later traded to the British in return for Russian spies.

second half of their 1914 offensive against the land of the Austro-Hungarian Empire, which shared a long border with lands controlled by Russia. The Russians struck at an area known as Galicia, which on today's map is split between Ukraine and Poland. Once an ancient kingdom, most of Galicia was controlled by Austria-Hungary at the outset of World War I.

In August the Austro-Hungarians struck first, driving into Poland and throwing the Russians on the defensive. The situation, however, was quickly reversed, and the Russians drove the Austro-Hungarians out of Poland and into Galicia. The Russians neatly trapped a large enemy army, just as the Germans had done to the Russians at Tannenberg. But the army fought its way out of the trap, and the Russian advance

ground to a halt due to a lack of supplies and poor organization.

This southern Russian advance proved to be an initial success and took pressure off Russian troops farther north on the eastern front, since the Germans moved troops south to help their ally defend against a Russian invasion. Once German troops arrived, however, the situation reversed. The Central Powers flung the Russians back. The fighting on the eastern front concentrated on Galicia for the rest of the war.

The Russian Army Begins to Crumble

In the spring of 1915, the Central Powers mounted an offensive in the region against worn Russian troops. The attack caused the Russians enormous losses and exhibited movement unseen on the western front since the beginning of the war. It is a marvel of German resourcefulness and industry that the Germans fought on two fronts, nearly breaking Allied armies on both. The Russians, for example, found themselves deprived of the war matériel they needed to defend against the German advance, especially field artillery and aircraft. "At the beginning of the war," wrote a Russian officer, "we had guns, ammunition, and rifles, we were victorious. When the supply of munitions and arms began to give out, we still fought brilliantly. Today . . . our army is drowning in its own blood."[34]

If Russia lacked in industrial supplies, however, it did not lack in manpower. Russia had the largest population of the nations at war. The size of the Russian army made up in part for its lack of artillery and other advanced weapons. At no time was this more evident than during the Brusilov offensive of 1916.

The offensive, named for the Russian commander Aleksey Brusilov, was a response to Allied appeals to take pressure off attacks on the western front and in Italy. The relentless German assault on Verdun and the continued fighting to the north caused the French to appeal to the Russians to launch at attack that would draw German forces away to the east. Czar Nicholas II responded by unleashing an assault against well-fortified positions in May. This attack was beaten off by determined German defenders, and in June the Russians decided to attack Austro-Hungarian positions farther south.

The Unraveling of Austria-Hungry

Even the Germans by this time considered the Austro-Hungarian positions their weak spot on the eastern front. German commanders replaced Austrian commanders, but Austria-Hungary was an empire on the decline. The empire had been stitched together by the Hapsburg dynasty and the royal family of Hungary out of a mishmash of central European peoples. Twin capitals at Vienna, Austria, and Budapest, Hungary, attempted to keep the diverse empire together, though Austria proved the senior partner in the dual government. By the outbreak of World War I, it was an empire already coming apart. Many of its subjects longed to form their own governments.

Unlike the kaiser's hungry appetite for prestige and land, the Austro-Hungarians had limited war aims. While the German policy was one of expansion, Austria-Hungary hoped only to keep its territory. They feared the loss of Balkan territories to Serbia. Some Austro-Hungarian lands had already been lost to Italy, and they feared the loss of more land around the Adriatic to the Italians, especially the prosperous city of Trieste, where many Italians lived.

The Austro-Hungarian forces spent most of the war fighting in the Balkans, holding back Russian advances on the eastern front, and fighting the Italians in the mountains that separated them.

A German soldier throws a hand grenade against enemy positions during World War I.

When the Italians added their voice to the Allied call for a Russian offensive in the spring and summer of 1916, the Russians decided to strike on a long front against Austro-Hungarian positions.

The Brusilov Offensive

In June Brusilov's army of more than half a million men struck along a 300-mile front (483km). It was an enormous area for an attack, but Brusilov's strategy was to probe for weak points while attacking strong points with specially trained assault troops. He also used surprise, sneaking troops up to enemy lines. Once his troops were in place, the Russians unleashed a furious artillery barrage up and down the front on June 4, 1916. The offensive caught the Austrians off guard, and at various places, Austrian troops retreated. The pent-up fury of the Russian soldiers caused them to pour through

The War of Snow and Ice

Between Austria and Italy runs the greatest natural barrier in Europe—the Alps. They are the highest mountains in Europe, and during the First World War formed one of the most unusual battlefields. While troops on the western front got bogged down in the mud and trenches of the plains of France and Belgium, soldiers in the Alps fought almost vertically.

Both Austria and Italy recruited mountaineers who knew the mountains well and put them into battle during the war. In Italy the Alpini, or Alpine mountaineer soldiers, became famous for their daring exploits in what became known as the "war of snow and ice." The Alpini and their Austrian counterparts struggled to hold the highest peaks, from which they could fire artillery down at their enemy. To counter gun emplacements or fortified positions on the snowy slopes, engineers often resorted to digging under the position and blowing it up with explosive charges, causing an avalanche and the fall of the strong point. The remains of soldiers from both sides still lie buried in the snow and ice today.

these gaps in the Austrian line with stunning speed. Within two days of the attack, the Austrian Fourth and Seventh armies retreated in confusion.

The Russians advanced in the north 50 miles (80.5km) into enemy territory and in the south 30 miles (48km). The Russian onslaught bogged down only when supplies failed to keep up with the troops. The Russians halted and picked up the offensive again in July and August. Brusilov had continued success, but as he moved farther into enemy territory, supplies became more of a problem and ammunition ran low. The pauses in the Brusilov offensive, moreover, allowed the Germans to move troops southward to shore up Austrian defenses. The Russian armies in the north also failed to

launch serious attacks on the German positions to prevent this. By the fall, the Russians had captured some four hundred thousand prisoners, but the offensive petered out in the face of stronger defenses and a lack of supplies.

The Brusilov offensive helped change the course of the war in two significant ways. The first was the complete exposure of the weaknesses of Austria-Hungary. Not only had its armies been routed, but some units had stopped fighting because they no longer believed in their government. Ethnic groups, neither Hungarian nor Austrian, could not see the point in fighting for foreign rulers, of whom they had grown tired anyway. Sensing the weakness of their ally, the Germans took command of the Austro-

Hungarian armies, dealing another blow to the pride of the once-great empire. Austria-Hungary after the Brusilov offensive survived only because the Germans held it together.

Revolution in Russia

The second momentous event resulting partly from the fierce fighting on the eastern front in 1916 was the Russian Revolution. Russian czar Nicholas I was the first to refer to the Ottoman Empire as the "sick man of Europe." The same could be said of the Russian Empire in the early twentieth century. Still largely an agrarian country, Russia in the early twentieth century struggled to become an industrialized nation. In 1905 crowds gathered in the Russian capital to protest the state of the economy and the rule of the czars, the imperial Russian rulers. The protest was put down violently by the Russian government, but discontent continued to simmer.

Russian suffering on the eastern front also caused resentment. Why did some get to remain comfortably in Russia, while so many millions of Russians suffered and died in battle? The soldiers also viewed many of their military leaders with skepticism, and many wondered just what they were fighting for.

Making the situation worse was the economic situation in Russia. As Russian factories got up and going to provide war supplies, some people made huge profits. Prices rose drastically and food became scarce, since farming did not produce the profits of factories or pay as high as factory labor. The food shortage prompted a protest against the government of Czar Nicholas II in February 1917. The czar became the focus of dissatisfaction and the inequalities in Russia. "The Emperor Nicholas II was a weak man," one historian concluded. "As commander in chief of the Russian armies he could not even fulfill the easiest task of an absolute monarch in war, that of arousing enthusiasm when he reviewed his troops."[35]

The February Revolution of 1917 succeeded in forcing the czar to give up his throne, and a provisional government

A food shortage in Russia prompted a protest against the government of Czar Nicholas II, pictured, in February 1917.

was set up under Alexander Kerensky, serving as prime minister. The new government also had a legislature, called the Duma, to allow Russians to participate in their government. Kerensky also served as the head of Russia's armies and continued to work with the Allies in the war effort. With the hardships of war and hunger, the Kerensky government failed to satisfy the unleashed discontent in Russian society.

The Rise of the Bolsheviks

Although Kerensky was himself a revolutionary, his government needed the rich industrialists to carry on the war. The wealthy, however, disapproved of revolution and hoped for a more conservative government. American journalist John Reed recorded the discontent among the wealthy in 1917 under the provisional government:

Winter was coming on—the terrible Russian winter. I heard businessmen speak of it so: "Winter was always Russia's best friend. Perhaps now it will rid us of Revolution." On the freezing front miserable armies continued to starve and die, without enthusiasm. The railways were breaking down, food lessening, factories closing. The desperate masses cried out that the bourgeoisie was sabotaging the life of the people, causing defeat on the Front.[36]

On the other hand, revolutionaries felt that the revolution had not gone far enough. The Bolsheviks, a Communist

The Archangel Expedition

Although the Bolsheviks signed a peace treaty with the Germans in 1918 effectively removing Russia from World War I, the fighting did not stop. German troops were still moving into parts of Russia, and anti-Bolshevik forces known as White Russians fought against the Russian Communists and hoped to continue the war against the Germans. White Russian forces still loyal to the former provisional government headed by Alexander Kerensky operated from bases in the far north of Russia along the White Sea.

In the hopes of propping up the eastern front and aiding White Russian forces against both the Germans and the Bolshevik government, the Allied Powers sent a military expedition to the port city of Archangel. American troops referred to the operation as the Polar Bear Expedition. Allied troops fought on after the end of World War I, but Soviet forces ultimately defeated the White Russians, and the Allies withdrew.

political movement, promised peace and bread, and many listened. "In this atmosphere of corruption, of monstrous half-truths, one clear note sounded day after day," wrote John Reed, "the deepening chorus of the Bolsheviki, 'All Power to the Soviets! All power to the direct representatives of millions on millions of common workers, soldiers, peasants. Land, bread, an end to the senseless war.'"[37]

According to the Bolshevik plan, the entire economy of Russia would be reorganized into soviets, or regional councils, that would give workers control over their government. The Bolsheviks offered Russians a new deal: no longer would the Russian people labor for the rich or remain voiceless in a government with no representation. They would also end the war and provide food for the hungry. Or at least that was the idea.

Vladimir Lenin, the most famous of the Bolsheviks, was in exile during the February Revolution. He spent most of the war in neutral Switzerland. The Germans, however, saw a use in sending Lenin back to Russia at this point. They put him in a sealed train, which was allowed to cross the eastern front and take him to Petrograd (now Saint Petersburg), the Russian capital. The Germans hoped that the revolution would cause Russia to pull out of the war. Despite protests from the Allies and accusations of treason in Russia, the Bolsheviks promised an immediate end to the war. One speaker responding heatedly to being called a defeatist outlined the Bolshevik position:

You call us defeatists; but the real defeatists are those who wait for a more propitious moment to conclude peace, insist on postponing peace until later, until nothing is left of the Russian army, until Russia becomes the subject of bargaining between the different imperialist groups. . . . You are trying to impose upon the Russian people a policy dictated by the interests of the bourgeoisie. The question of peace should be raised without delay.[38]

On November 8, 1917, the Russian Soviet Congress, which had swept aside the Kerensky government, elected Lenin as the new ruler of Soviet Russia. Lenin advocated immediate peace with the Germans, but other Bolsheviks refused to surrender. While the Bolsheviks argued, the Germans advanced. Their interference in Russian politics had finished what they had started on the battlefield—the collapse of Russia's defenses. The German army marched 150 miles (241km) into Russian territory within a week in mid-February 1918.

Russia Sues for Peace

Quickly losing vast stretches of territory to the Central Powers, the Bolshevik government agreed to peace terms in the treaty of Brest-Litovsk, named for a town now called Brest in Belarus where the negotiators met, effectively taking Russia out of World War I. War on the eastern front contributed to the collapse of this second great empire, after Austria-Hungary. The implications for the war were enormous.

This now-famous military recruiting poster was created after the United States declared war on Germany and entered World War I on April 6, 1917.

The collapse of the eastern front freed German troops to move to other fronts. German troops marched toward Italy, where the Austrians had managed throughout the war to hold back the larger Italian army. Geography played a key role, since the mountains often allowed the Austrians to take up positions on high ground and defend against Italian attacks.

The Germans also traveled to the western front, generally speeding along on good German railways. The danger to the Allies was tremendous. Since 1914 Germany had managed to conduct a two-front war. Although it did not provide the quick victory the kaiser had hoped for, it did show that the German army could fight on two fronts and not be beaten. With Russia removed from the war, Germany finally had the chance to mobilize the greater bulk of its armies against the Allies on the western front.

Exhaustion and discontent plagued the Allied armies on the western front, and now they were forced to prepare for possibly the decisive offensive of the war. And then the news came—the United States had abandoned neutrality and declared war on Germany. Artillery, planes, and many other industrial products needed for modern war were in short supply in America. But the Allies needed above all the soldiers—soldiers to fill the gaps in Allied defenses and to restore confidence.

Despite the many other fronts in World War I, in Turkey and in the Middle East, and the battles at sea and overhead, the outcome of the war would be determined in Europe, where it had begun. Georges Clemenceau, the leader of France, outlined the situation at a meeting in 1918 of the Allied Supreme War Council, which directed the Allied war effort: "The Security of the western front overrode all other considerations. The Treason of Russia (he used the word deliberately) had exposed the Allies to the greatest danger they had yet met. His plan was to hold out this year, 1918, till the American assistance came in full force; after that America would win the war."[39]

Chapter Five

America on the March

The United States took a long and tortured path toward entry into World War I. The United States generally believed that the squabbles of European nations should be left to the Europeans to sort out. The policy of U.S. president Woodrow Wilson was to stay out of the war, but perhaps to act as a broker of peace. He saw America's role as a moral role, to set an example for the rest of the world, and he proclaimed that the United States was "too proud to fight."[40]

The desire to remain aloof from the conflicts of other nations stretched back to early American history. On becoming president in 1801, Thomas Jefferson proclaimed this tendency—known as isolationism: "Peace, commerce and honest friendship with all nations, entangling alliances with none, I deem the essential principles of our government." Jefferson, like George Washington and the other founding fathers of the American repub-lic, was most concerned with establishing an identity separate from Europe. "Our first and fundamental maxim should be never to entangle ourselves in the broils of Europe,"[41] Jefferson said.

Yet the United States had changed greatly from those early days. While Jefferson worried about the establishment of a new republic, Woodrow Wilson during World War I worried more about the role of an already established power in the community of nations. Indeed, many Americans felt that the United States should join the Allied cause. They had many reasons. Europe was the source of America's democratic political traditions. The French had aided America during the American Revolution. And many Americans of English heritage longed to assist the British. Some Americans volunteered to fight in the years before the United States entered the war. They fought in the Canadian, British, and French armies and generally hoped that their government would follow them into the war.

The war also had many advocates in U.S. politics. Former president Theodore Roosevelt, for example, became a harsh critic of Wilson's neutrality policy. "It is well to remember," he said, "that there are things worse than war."[42]

Unrestricted Submarine Warfare

The Germans ultimately provided cause enough to swing opinion in the United States toward a declaration of war on Germany. When a German submarine torpedoed the *Lusitania* in 1915, killing 1,195 passengers, including 123 Americans, the United States had come very close to declaring war on Germany. In the end, it was once again the feared U-boat, so menacing to transatlantic shipping, that turned opinion in America.

After the sinking of the *Lusitania*, Germany had stopped sinking ships without warning in the North Atlantic for fear of provoking war with the United States. In the spring of 1917, however, the Germans were feeling the bite of the British blockade of Germany and decided to try to starve Britain by sinking ships carrying supplies to the British Isles. The Germans knew that the resumption of this policy would lead to the sinking of American

Attacks on civilians by German U-boats were largely responsible for Americans deciding to abandon neutrality and enter World War I.

ships, and they expected war with America. They reasoned, however, that they could prevent the landing of U.S. troops by sinking ships transporting them across the Atlantic.

To this menacing policy, the Germans added a plot to give Mexico the former Mexican territories that had become the states of Texas, Arizona, and New Mex-

Lafayette Escadrille

O f the American volunteers who fought in World War I before the United States declared war, the most famous are the pilots of the Lafayette Escadrille. These American fliers flew French planes under French command. They served, however, as a unit, first known as the Escadrille Américaine, or American Flying Corps. The group was later renamed in honor of the Marquis de Lafayette, a French aristocrat who had volunteered to fight in the American War of Independence.

The squadron was formed in April 1916, a year before the United States entered the war. The pilots adorned their planes with the unit's insignia—an American Indian war chief. They saw combat in the Battle of Verdun, where they supported French troops from the air. After the United States declared war in 1917, the Lafayette Escadrille was incorporated into the U.S. Army Air Service.

Edward F. Hinkel, member of the Lafayette Escadrille, was an American volunteer who fought in World War I before the United States officially entered the war.

ico. The Germans hoped to stall U.S. entry into the war by sparking a war between Mexico and the United States. This plot was hatched by Arthur Zimmermann, the German foreign secretary, and transmitted to Mexico by telegram. British intelligence picked up the transmission and eagerly passed it on to the U.S. president. The British hoped that at long last the United States would join the Allied war effort.

The Zimmermann Telegram

On March 1, 1917, the telegram, known to history as the Zimmermann telegram, was published in an American newspaper. Not only did the telegram state Germany's intention to resume submarine warfare against unarmed neutral ships in the Atlantic Ocean, but it also indicated that it would support a Mexican invasion of the United States. For Senator Henry Cabot Lodge of Massachusetts, a withering critic of Wilson's neutrality stance, the telegram provided ammunition to fire against Wilson and public support of neutrality: "As soon as I saw it, I felt it would arouse the country more than anything else that has happened."[43]

Some at first did not believe the news. They thought it might be a trick by the Allies to draw America to war. People looked to Washington to confirm that the telegram was genuine. "If the President could be got to say it was authentic, at one stroke he would be 'tied up,'" Barbara Tuchman writes in her history of the telegram. "He would have given the country a national reason to be enraged at Germany and be unable to dissociate himself from the result. He had provided, gloated [Henry Cabot] Lodge, the very instrument that would be of 'almost unlimited use in forcing the situation.'"[44]

From Wilson's point of view, the Germans had indeed gone too far. The telegram and its indications that German U-boats would attack unarmed U.S. ships required action. The United States declared war on April 6, 1917.

America Enters the Fray

The Germans were wrong on two important points in this gamble. First, Mexico did not desire war with the United States, and second, German submarines were unable to prevent U.S. soldiers from reaching Europe. By war's end, over 2 million American soldiers had crossed the Atlantic, providing fresh troops to the Allied forces.

The troops were slow in coming, however. Georges Clemenceau's remark that the Americans would win the war once they arrived in force was a generous assessment. While the U.S. Navy ranked second only to Britain's, its army ranked seventeenth in the world. In the atmosphere of isolationism under President Wilson, there had been few real preparations for war. General John J. Pershing, com-

Army recruits answer the call to war in New York soon after President Woodrow Wilson declared war on Germany in 1917.

mander in chief of the American Expeditionary Force, bemoaned the lack of war preparations. "The fact that when we entered the war our Government had done little or nothing toward the organization or equipment of an army," he wrote, "not to mention its transportation beyond the sea, was a tremendous handicap which few of our people realized then."[45]

Although it would take the United States nearly a year to mobilize, the president ordered Pershing to sail to Europe with a small advance army. They paraded in Paris on the Fourth of July, 1917. The effect on morale was enormous. After years of battering, the Allies received a vast reserve of fresh troops. A fierce debate over how best to use the troops, however, broke out at once. French general Ferdinand Foch, who was made overall commander of the Allied forces, wanted to use American soldiers to reinforce British and French lines.

The Debate over How to Use the Troops

The Americans had come, but they lacked the arms and equipment needed for battle, and the troops in the front desperately needed bodies. The French supplied the American Expeditionary Force with arms but balked at giving the Americans artillery to use in their own offensive. "The object of the Entente [Allied cooperation] was to obtain an indispensable superiority in numbers," French commander Marshal Foch wrote in his memoirs, "and it would scarcely have accorded with its interests to deprive French units of their artillery for the benefit of American units."[46]

Pershing compromised. He integrated some American units into Allied armies until U.S. soldiers could arrive in force, when they would serve as a separate army. American soldiers first moved into French trenches in October 1917. As a point of national pride, the soldiers were determined to show the bravery of U.S. fighting men. It took time, however, for them to be accustomed to the strange, brutish world of the trenches. "I shot six

An American soldier throws a hand grenade during fighting in Aneauville, France, in 1918. The infusion of U.S. troops boosted morale on the battlefield.

Harlem's Hell Fighters

During World War I, racial discrimination kept African American soldiers out of regular fighting units in the army. Volunteers from New York formed the all-black 369th Infantry Regiment, commonly known as Harlem's Hell Fighters. The regiment was attached to French forces in 1918 and fought in the Second Battle of the Marne. They distinguished themselves for their bravery, and in the advance to Germany became the first American regiment to reach the Rhine River.

Germans sneaking up on me one night," wrote one soldier, "and when daylight came they were all the same [tree] stump."[47]

The initial effect of the arrival of U.S. troops was on Allied morale. After years in the trenches, the Allied forces found the optimism and enthusiasm of new soldiers refreshing. "The impression made upon the hard-pressed French by this seemingly inexhaustible flood of gleaming youth in its first maturity of health and vigour was prodigious,"[48] wrote Winston Churchill on the arrival of the Americans. Their military use came the following spring, when they began to function as an army and take part in the fierce spring fighting that followed a particularly harsh winter.

Germany's Spring Offensive

For the Germans the year 1918 was supposed to be one of great victory. They hoped to punch through the Allied lines on the western front in the early spring

before U.S. troops had arrived in force. They intended to make use of German troops freed from the eastern front and of new battle tactics. General Oskar von Hutier had come up with new methods of attack intended to penetrate Allied defenses. Hutier theorized that specially trained shock troops could spearhead an attack, which would then be followed by masses of ground infantry. German officers of all levels would have more freedom to order offensive action to exploit weak points in the Allied defensive lines. The German army set about training soldiers in the techniques, and in the massive German spring offensive, they set them loose.

The Germans first attacked on March 21, 1918, against British defenses in France near the Somme River, where Allied forces had made a particularly bloody advance in 1916. The Germans threw a million men into the offensive. British positions crumbled, and the Germans gained 40 miles (64km) before the Allies could regroup. Hutier's tactics seemed a proven success, and the Germans followed up their initial victories with attacks elsewhere along the western front.

In early April German forces used the same tactics against Allied positions near the Leie River, which runs through France and Belgium. The British under General Douglas Haig, who had replaced John French as the commander in chief of the British Expeditionary Force, prepared to retreat to the coast, even as he tried to bolster defenses and stop the Germans.

U.S. Troops in the Fight

In June the Germans attacked Allied positions father south, and in July they attacked at the Marne, the sight of so much bloodshed at the outbreak of the war. The Allies retreated in many places along the line. The war seemed once again to become a war of motion, as old trenches were overrun and troops fought running battles, at least until they could dig in again. In the southern sector, the Germans made their longest advance since the beginning of the war. They drove the Allies back toward the town of Château-Thierry, only 50 miles (80.5km) from Paris.

As the French retreated, they met American troops coming up to support the Allied defenses. U.S. marines, the most well trained of American soldiers, saw battle for the first time since arriving in France. American troops attacked German positions in Belleau Wood, a forest area near the Marne, and learned the painful lessons of attacking machine-gun positions head on. Many died, but their bravery lived up to their traditional pride. They captured their objective after a week of fighting and heavy losses.

The Battle of Belleau Wood proved the worth of the fresh American troops. It also helped stop the German advance. The military significance of the position was slight, but the battle helped further erode German morale. Despite the enormous gains of the Germans in their spring offensive, things were not going well. As the Germans pushed through Allied lines, they found the front getting only bigger and could not exploit their gains. Moreover, the shock troops that successfully led the assaults all along the line suffered heavily. By midsummer, many of these troops had been killed. In fact, thousands of Germans died in the advances. The German tactics worked, but to what end? They possessed a few more miles of France, but had failed to destroy the Allied armies. They had lost thousands of men in the offensives, and many more had grown weary of the endless fighting. German discipline, so impressive for much of the war, slipped. The German offensive stalled in July 1918.

The Swing of the Pendulum

As the German offensive lost momentum, the Allies counterattacked. It was almost as if a giant pendulum had swung forward, stalled at its highest point, and begun to swing back again, gaining momentum. At the Marne, where American troops had helped clear Belleau Wood, the defense against the German attack became a counteroffensive without a pause in the fighting.

A wounded U.S. marine receives flowers from a Frenchwoman following the battle of Belleau Wood in 1918.

On July 18 Allied Supreme Commander Ferdinand Foch ordered a gigantic thrust to hurl the Germans back. French troops, augmented by thousands of U.S. soldiers supported by tanks, cut through the exhausted Germans. By the time the offensive ground to a halt, the Germans had lost all the gains they made in the area during the spring offensive. It was a major victory. Not only had the Allies survived the most ferocious attack the Germans could muster, but they also proved that they could beat German armies in the field.

Foch wrote of the importance of the Second Battle of the Marne, as this counteroffensive became known, in his memoirs:

Above all, the morale of the German Army had been lowered, that of the Allies raised. After four months on the defensive, imposed upon us by the enemy's numerical superiority, a victorious counter offensive had once more placed in our hands the initiative of operations and the power to direct the progress of events in this long, vast war.[49]

The Second Battle of the Marne proved to be a turning point in the war. Foch seized the initiative and displayed his grasp of overall strategy. He ordered attacks all along the line, probing for soft

The large-scale introduction of tanks into the fighting during the Second Battle of the Marne allowed the Allies to begin to turn the tide against the Germans.

spots in the German line. In the north the British attacked near the French city of Amiens. Tanks, invented by the British, heartened the soldiers as they advanced. Hundreds of tanks were now in service, and they caught defenders off guard. The Germans simply lacked the weapons to destroy them, and the sight of a lumber-ing steel giant approaching with a large muzzle gun and machine guns caused them to retreat. As the British pushed forward, the Germans fell back. The war had once again become a war of maneuver. Large armies attempted to outmaneuver each other in a race for good positions.

Closing in on Germany

While the British attacked in the north, the French and American troops continued to gain ground in the south. U.S. forces flowing into France by the thousands could now field large armies. To the south, in an area where the Germans had pushed the Allied line westward, U.S. troops launched an offensive on September 12, 1918, in coordination with the French. The area was known as the Saint Mihiel salient, south of the French battleground of Verdun.

Airpower assisted the American advance. Pershing had ordered thousands of planes from the French. The planes were piloted by Americans trained by fliers who had flown as volunteers before the United States entered the war. "Fortunately, some ninety of these experienced American fliers who had thus volunteered in the French Army from 1914 to 1917 joined our aviation, and their services as instructors and in combat proved of inestimable value to us."[50]

With the airplanes overhead and the tanks battering through defensive positions, trench warfare was quickly becoming obsolete. The American offensive eliminated the German bulge in the line. General Erich Ludendorf, who had planned the spring offensive, ordered troops to fall back and dig in to new defensive positions.

The Allies had no desire to let the Germans rest, however. On September 25, 1918, the British launched a major offensive near Cambrai, driving toward Belgium. On the same day, a major French-American offensive opened in the Argonne Forest, north of Verdun. The terrain made for tough fighting. Troops got lost in the forests, and soldiers stumbled upon each other. American troops took heavy casualties, but the advance continued to drive the Germans northward in October. "The period of the battle from October 1st to the 11th involved the heaviest strain on the army and on me,"[51] General Pershing wrote.

One of the great problems for an army advancing quickly on a retreating army was the ease of an ambush. German units could stop, set up machine guns and artillery, and hold off attackers as the rest of the army slipped farther away. In fact, Foch's greatest anxiety during the successful Allied offensives of the fall of 1918 was that the German army would fall back and regroup, and the static trench warfare would start again:

> Ever since the middle of the month of August [1918] I had been worried by the fear that the German Commander in Chief might extricate his armies from our grip and abruptly break off the combat in order to resume it some distance in the rear. Here he could select better positions on a shorter front, behind obstacles and on ground more favourable to the defensive and make a new distribution of his forces such as might enable him to launch an advantageous counter attack.[52]

In October 1918 the Allied armies advanced in three prongs, north, center, and south, along the western front. After lingering for so long in the trenches, the armies closed in on Germany itself. At this point, political factors took over. The Ottoman Empire surrendered in October. Austria-Hungary, that giant combination of various ethnic groups, split apart. The Italians advanced into land long held by Austrian forces, and the various peoples of Austria-Hungary declared their independence from the crumbling empire. The Austrians, at the heart of the empire, surrendered to the Italians in the first week of November. The Hungarians declared their independence, ending the ancient association

American soldiers stand outside a captured enemy dugout at the western front in October 1918, less than a month before Germany surrendered.

Armored Water Carriers

When war on the western front bogged down in stalemate and soldiers dug into the trenches, offensives became brutally costly. Artillery, barbed wire, and machine guns guarded the trenches on both sides. Both sides worked frantically for a new weapon that could break the deadlock.

An officer of the British Royal Engineers, Frank Swinton, believed he had the solution. He drew up outlines for an armored truck that could drive through barbed wire and repel bullets. The British produced the first of these new weapons, destined to change warfare forever. To keep the weapon a secret, they shipped them to continental Europe in crates marked "tanks," and soldiers referred to the lumbering armored beasts as "water carriers."

The British first used the tank in the Battle of the Somme in 1916. It terrified defenders in the trenches, who had no weapon to stop it. The tanks, however, had mechanical problems and often got stuck in the mud. By war's end improved tanks could drive across trenches, punching through lines that had remained stagnant for so long.

with Austria. Everywhere, it seemed, the Central Powers were collapsing.

Germany Breaks

This was no less true in Germany. Hunger and war weariness stalked the German people. They took to the streets in protest against the kaiser and his war. New political parties called for an end to the German Empire and the founding of a German republic. Many soldiers too had had enough. When Admiral Hipper ordered the German High Seas Fleet out in the autumn of 1918, the sailors mutinied. There would be no more fighting at sea.

The army held, not ready to surrender its pride. The kaiser, on the other hand, lost his nerve. He fled to the Netherlands on November 10, 1918, where he lived in exile for the rest of his life. His ambition to make the German Empire the equal of Great Britain and to win fame as a great war leader had led only to ruin in Germany and the end of the monarchy. No king has since taken the throne in Germany. Revolution was on the march, and Germany's new leaders scrambled to put together a more moderate government.

The day after the kaiser abandoned Germany, a German delegation traveled to a spot in France where the Germans had delivered humiliating peace terms to the French after their war in 1871. At 11 A.M., guns all along the western front fell silent. For France, where so much of the fighting had taken place, it was a bittersweet moment. They had won, and they would regain their beloved lands of Alsace and Lorraine. They had avenged the defeat of 1871, but large swaths of French territory were a wasteland. There would be little sympathy for Germany in the peace negotiations that were to be held the following year at the French city of Versailles on the outskirts of Paris.

French leader Georges Clemenceau believed that a harsh peace should follow Germany's brutal war: "The most terrible balancing of accounts between peoples has begun. The account will be paid. . . . Our dead gave their blood in witness that we took up the greatest challenge ever offered to the laws of civilized humanity. Let it be then, as Germany has willed it, as Germany has made it."[53]

Chapter Six

Versailles and After

The peace negotiations that followed World War I are as much a part of the history of the war as the battlefield fighting. The peace treaty was intended to settle many of the issues over which the war was fought. Some 10 million soldiers died in the war, and more than 20 million suffered from war wounds. About 22 million civilians also died. Europeans spoke of a lost generation of young men.

The war also caused momentous political changes. It toppled four empires—the German, Austro-Hungarian, Ottoman, and Russian. At the end of the war, Germans were starving. Civil war raged in Russia and Turkey (the center of the former Ottoman Empire). Huge swaths of France were unlivable and the farming and industry in the area ruined. What had it all been for?

And what would the postwar world look like?

'The "Big Four" Allies congregate at the Versailles peace conference in 1919. From left to right are David Lloyd George of Great Britain, Vittorio Orlando of Italy, Georges Clemenceau of France, and Woodrow Wilson of the United States.

The Paris Peace Conference

These were the questions to be addressed at the Paris Peace Conference, which lasted for six months from January to June 1919. Delegations from the nations of the world—and from people who hoped to found a nation—traveled to Paris. In fact, it seemed that representatives from the whole world descended on the French capital. The victorious Allies, who controlled the proceedings, perhaps came as close to a world government as has ever been seen in history. They drew up new maps for parts of Europe, Asia, Africa, and the Middle East. They listened to the delegations arguing their positions and ruled on them like judges in a court. Sometimes they made rulings based on fairness, sometimes on logic, and sometimes on emotion alone. At times, they made decisions that would benefit only themselves.

When the Germans agreed to the armistice of November 11, 1918, they believed that they had agreed to negotiate peace terms. They thought they would argue over the future of Germany, though admittedly from the position of a country whose leaders had been beaten. Nevertheless, they believed they would be able to argue their case in Paris. This was not to be. It is important to realize that the agonizing decisions made in Paris in the six months of 1919 were made by the Allied Powers alone. The Germans were not consulted, and never would be.

Over what, then, did the Allies have to argue? Had they not fought with the common war aim of defeating the Central Powers and securing the safety of their own nations? The answer is yes and no. The Allied Powers had very different ideas on how the world should look after the war. The great drama of the peace negotiations played out not between the Allied and Central Powers—the victors and the vanquished—but between the Allies themselves.

France, Britain, and the United States formed the big three of the negotiations at Paris. Italy, at times included with the three great powers, sometimes made for a big four, who made the main decisions of the peace. When the Germans agreed to an armistice, they had based their hopes on the principles of U.S. president Woodrow Wilson. After avoiding war until 1917, Wilson declared before a joint session of the U.S. Congress that the world must be made safe for democracy:

> We shall fight for the things which we have always carried nearest our hearts—for democracy, for the right of those who submit to authority to have a voice in their own governments, for the rights and liberties of small nations, for a universal dominion of right by such a concert of free peoples as shall bring peace and safety to all nations and make the world itself at last free.[54]

The American Peace Position

These were noble ideas befitting the American republic, which had fought for its own democratic rights and won independence

The people of Paris celebrate the declared armistice and the end of World War I in November 1918.

from the British Empire through revolution. Wilson outlined his ambitions in his famous Fourteen Points. Above all, they emphasized that the future of the peoples of the world should be determined by those peoples themselves. The Allies would become the midwives for the birth of new nations. Political boundaries would be redrawn to represent only the wishes of the peoples in those countries.

Some of the Fourteen Points were very specific. The ancient state of Poland, lingering under domination from the Austro-Hungarian Empire, should re-emerge as an independent country. All troops should leave Belgium, the invasion of which had outraged the world in 1914. Other points were deceptively simple. In point five, Wilson called for "a free, open-minded, and absolutely impartial adjustment of all colonial claims."[55] Just what, however, did that mean? Were all colonies to be granted independence as newly formed countries?

The Allies would debate the practicality of Wilson's Fourteen Points, but on his arrival to Paris, he was hailed almost as a prophet. All the hope and optimism for a new world seemed to be placed on the shoulders of the American president. They cheered him in France, and through the newspapers of the world. The American program offered a new way of ordering world affairs.

According to Wilson's ideas, the countries would be redrawn on the map by

The Mysterious Mr. House

The Paris Peace Conference welcomed advisers and experts from around the world. For the most part, the negotiations were directed by the leaders of France, Great Britain, Italy, and the United States. Each nation's leader was accompanied by experts in foreign affairs. The American delegation included Robert Lansing, the secretary of state, or director of United States foreign policy. Lansing soon found, however, that his advice was often ignored and that President Woodrow Wilson listened instead to another adviser, who held no official government post in the United States. This was Colonel Edward M. House.

House, who was always known as Colonel House even though he was not a colonel, had backed Wilson for president in 1911. After Wilson was elected, House became his closest adviser and even lived in the White House. House became a major international figure and chief negotiator for the U.S. delegation to the Paris Peace Conference. He finally broke with Wilson toward the end of the conference because of their bickering over the treaty terms, and the extraordinary friendship came to an end.

language groups or ethnic groups. The Austro-Hungarian Empire had already broken into two separate countries, Austria and Hungary. And from the ruins of the empire, other nations would emerge—Czechoslovakia, Balkan nations, Poland, and Ukraine. Likewise, from the old Ottoman lands in the Middle East would arise new Arab countries, free at last to determine their own future.

Disunity Among the Allied Powers

Wilson's plan, however, alarmed the other Allied Powers. Britain and France still had empires to run, and Italy had joined the Allied cause with no greater objective than seizing more land for Italy. If the British and French were to adopt Wilson's program, what would happen to their empires? Having fought since 1914, the French and British considered Wilson to be a latecomer to the war effort. While they needed U.S. troops in the war, they hardly welcomed his suggestion that colonies should be given a choice to form independent nations.

Traditionally, lands seized from a nation defeated at war were divided between the victors. Wilson wanted none of this. The British and the French, however, had started dividing up the spoils of war even before the war ended. After taking power in Russia, the Bolsheviks published secret treaties signed by the British and French dividing the Middle East between themselves. The Sykes-Picot Agreement, the name of the secret agreement to divide former Ottoman lands, would give Britain sway in Mesopotamia (present-day Iraq), Palestine (present-day Israel and the Palestinian territories), and Jordan; and France the lands of Syria, including Lebanon, and part of Turkey. For the French and British, land in the Middle East was the just prize for winning the war.

A British officer serving in the Palestine campaign concluded after meeting with King George V that the king had no intention of relinquishing land captured from the Central Powers. "He seemed to take it for granted that German East Africa, Palestine and Mesopotamia would come under the British Crown at the end of the war. . . . He particularly desired Palestine for biblical reasons. He made some remarks about the final crusade."[56]

Not only had Wilson in the first of his Fourteen Points called for "open covenants of peace, openly arrived at,"[57] but the secret treaties also contradicted wartime guarantees of the Allied Powers. On November 7, 1918, for example, the British and French published a joint

President Woodrow Wilson acknowledges the crowds that greet him during a campaign to gain support for the League of Nations.

statement of their intention to support independent governments in the Middle East:

> The goal envisaged by France and Great Britain in prosecuting in the East the war set in train by the German ambition is the complete and final liberation of the peoples who have for so long been oppressed by the Turks, and the setting up of national governments and administrations that shall derive their authority from the free exercise of the initiative and choice of the indigenous populations.[58]

The League of Nations

The Allies appeared to be playing a double game—at once promising independence for new nations and hoping to expand their own influence through new colonies. Wilson opposed this line entirely. But there was a single point among his Fourteen Points that Wilson held more dearly than all the others. It was in fact the last on his list, and it called for an association of nations to guarantee the rights of smaller nations in the future and to prevent war. This association was named the League of Nations. In Wilson's view, the war had been caused by secret treaties, greed, and the bullying of larger powers. The League of Nations would prevent future wars by openly protecting smaller nations and settling international disputes. It was a radical, far-thinking idea.

The French leader, Georges Clemenceau, and the British prime minister David Lloyd George, realized how dearly Wilson held the League of Nations plan. Both leaders showed considerably more skill at the give and take of debate. They used Wilson's attachment to the league plan to get him to compromise on other subjects. The peace conference became a grand haggling over the future of large parts of the globe.

Wilson agreed, for example, to the division of influence between Britain and France in the Middle East, but only if the territories would be governed under the League of Nations. By this plan, the British and French would have a League of Nations mandate to guide the new nations toward self-government. Of course, a central part of colonization was always the promise that the lands would be handed over to the people when they were mature. Wilson, in fact, was agreeing to new colonies under a different name.

The Arabs, who had fought alongside the Allied cause against the Turks, felt betrayed. Some of the British officers who served with them felt ashamed of Britain's treatment of a wartime ally. "We lived many lives in those whirling campaigns, never sparing ourselves: yet when we achieved and the new world dawned, the old men came out again and took our victory to re-make in the likeness of the former world they knew,"[59] wrote Thomas Edward Lawrence, who fought with the Arabs.

As the peace conference progressed, Wilson conceded to ever more trade-offs to retain support for the League of Nations. It was as if the U.S. president sacrificed the short term for the future. In

Faisal (foreground), soon to become king of Syria and Iraq, with his delegates and advisers at the Paris Peace Conference in 1919. Colonel T. E. Lawrence is in the second row, second from right. Some of the British officers who served with the Arabs during the war felt ashamed of Britain's treatment of them during the peace negotiations.

the future, the League of Nations, he hoped, would prevent war and mark a new age of international relations. In the short term, compromises had to be made. Nowhere was this more apparent than the debate over the Chinese province of Shandong.

Japanese delegates joined the Council of Ten, the main decision-making body at the peace negotiations, as equals of the other great powers—France, Great Britain, the United States, and Italy (each

had two delegates, making for a council of ten). Japan was a rising power with a strong navy. The Japanese had played only a minor role in the war, but for their support of the league plan, Wilson agreed to their demands at Paris.

The Case of Shandong

The Japanese wanted the former German colony of Qingdao on the Shandong Peninsula. The Chinese, of course, wanted their territory back. Not only did the

Chinese have the legal claim to the area, since it was indisputably part of China, but they had also supported the Allied Powers in the war. Chinese workers sailed from the Far East and supported Allied troops on the western front by working behind the lines, moving supplies and helping transport them. The Chinese responded to the Japanese claim to Shandong with outrage.

American opinion generally sided with the Chinese, and even members of the American delegation at the peace conference believed that the United States could not in good faith agree to the Japanese demand. General Tasker H. Bliss, a member of the American delegation, said in a letter to President Wilson:

If we support Japan's claim, we abandon the democracy of China to the domination of the Prussianized militarism of Japan.

We shall be sowing dragons' teeth.

It can't be right to do wrong even to make peace. Peace is desirable, but there are things dearer than peace, justice and freedom.[60]

Robert Lansing, U.S. secretary of state and a peace commissioner on the American delegation to Paris, believed that Wilson was sacrificing basic U.S. principles to secure support for the League of Nations: "Our chief differences were,

Chinese refugees flee war-ravaged Shandong, taken over by the Japanese with Allied approval after World War I. The controversial decisions made by the Allies during the peace process would eventually undermine the credibility of the West among nations in East Asia, the Middle East and Africa.

Mapping the Modern Middle East

The collapse of the Ottoman Empire in 1918 left huge swaths of the Middle East without a government. For centuries foreign invaders had crossed this area, which lies at the intersection of Asia, Europe, and Africa.

Turkey, the center of the former Ottoman Empire, became a republic and abandoned all claims to the Middle Eastern lands. The map of the Middle East that we know today was drawn up by the French and British in the years following World War I. The French controlled the ancient Roman province of Syria, and eventually Lebanon broke away and formed its own independent country.

The British awarded their wartime ally the Hashemite family the kingdoms of Trans-Jordan (present-day Jordan) and Iraq, though the Hashemite leader of Iraq, King Faisal, was later overthrown. In the heart of Saudi Arabia, a warlike desert leader named Ibn Saud founded his own nation, today known as Saudi Arabia.

first, that it was more important to insure the acceptance of the Covenant of the League of Nations than to do strict justice to China; second, that the Japanese withdrawal from the Conference would prevent the formation of the League; and, third, that Japan would have withdrawn if her claims had been denied."[61]

Japan, however, was not denied its claim and eventually won support for its possession of Chinese territory. The Japanese in subsequent years moved farther into Chinese territory and attempted eventually to dominate China entirely. In China the Treaty of Versailles was treated as evidence that the Western powers would support a fellow military power over a fellow democracy. Just as the war had so eroded the admiration all over the world of Western civilization, the peace treaty that followed further undermined the credibility of the West among nations in East Asia, the Middle East, and Africa.

What to Do with the Colonies

Despite the anticolonial nature of Wilson's Fourteen Points, he compromised on most of the colonial questions, and both the French and British empires expanded after the war. The Japanese Empire, which the Allied Powers would fight in World War II, also grew in strength and territory from the peace terms decided at Paris in 1919.

Yet because of the open discussions on colonies and because of Wilson's support for self-determination—the right of people everywhere to decide what kind of government they wanted—discontent in colonies around the globe grew steadily. World War I is thus credited with speeding the end of the colonial system.

The Allied Powers did considerably better in Europe. The collapse of the Austro-Hungarian and Ottoman empires allowed for many countries to form their own governments. Poland, for example, which for so long had been controlled by foreign powers, reemerged as an independent country. An army of linguists, mapmakers, and historians attempted to regroup people based on common language and ethnicity.

Bargaining over Germany's Fate

When the Allies took up the question of Germany, the disputes among the big three once again flared up. The future of Germany, the cause of so much suffering in the world war, sparked a fierce debate. The French, who shared a border with Germany and had been invaded, understandably wanted Germany treated harshly. The French also wanted to make sure the German army could not strike again.

Above all, two factors proved difficult to agree upon. France wanted the Allies to occupy the Rhineland, a part of Germany that bordered France, and Germany to pay for the war. According to the French, the Germans must be demilitarized. Their army would be reduced to a small force, and no submarines or warplanes would be allowed. The occupation of German territory would ensure the safety of France. "America is far away, protected by the ocean. Even Napoleon could not reach England," Clemenceau argued to Wilson and Lloyd George. "You are both under cover. We

are not. No man has less of the militaristic spirit than I. But we want safety."[62]

The British and Americans agreed, principally out of deference to France. The Allies also wanted the Germans to repay the costs of the war in payments known as reparations. Great Britain, however, feared that France would dominate the European continent if Germany was crippled with war debt. The United States also hoped that the German economy would get up and running as soon as possible. Wilson had called for a peace without victory as the war aim of the United States. He took the long view that a strong, democratic Germany would make war in Europe less likely in the future.

The Allies could not agree, but the Germans would certainly be required to send much of the fruits of their national industry to the Allied Powers over the coming years. The question of reparations was ultimately put off for a post-peace convention. This made the Germans extremely uneasy. They were signing a document that required them to pay their enemies an undetermined amount of money over an undetermined period of time. "The German people would thus be condemned to perpetual slave labour,"[63] remarked one of the German delegates to the peace conference.

The German government was so upset by the peace terms that they refused to sign. This set off a crisis in Germany, and a new government was formed. From the Allied point of view, Germany must either sign or resume fighting. The new German government sent representatives by train to Germany to sign without negotiations. The Germans would have no say in the peace terms.

The Paris Peace Conference concluded on June 28, 1919, with the signing of the treaty in the ornate Hall of Mirrors at the Palace of Versailles, a short distance outside of Paris. Delegates streamed into the palace, and newspaper correspondents and throngs of spectators hovered outside. Everyone wanted to catch a glimpse of this momentous historic event. For two figures in particular, however, it was a black day. The German foreign minister Hermann Müller and Johannes Bell, the colonial secretary of a Germany stripped of colonies, represented Germany at the ceremony.

After the war with France in 1871, the Germans had chosen the Hall of Mirrors to announce the founding of the German Empire. Now Müller and Bell signed a treaty that symbolized defeat for Germany in the same symbolic place. "This is a great day for France,"[64] remarked Georges Clemenceau, who presided over the signing. In Germany it was a day of mourning. The feeling in Germany was that the treaty was unfair. People felt that

The German army complies with the terms of the Treaty of Versailles and begins the process of disarming, turning in their weapons and other war matériel in 1920.

the terms of the treaty would ruin Germany. Above all, it injured German pride, just as French pride was wounded after the defeat of 1871.

A Peace to End All Peace

The Treaty of Versailles was ratified by the League of Nations, which came into being after the war, just as Woodrow Wilson had hoped. Not all, however, agreed that an international body was the best way to solve the world's problems. Chief among the critics was the U.S. Congress, which refused to ratify the Treaty of Versailles and refused to join the League of Nations. Wilson failed in the end to convince his own countrymen of his dream for a better world. The League limped on until World War II but never managed to solve international disputes as it was intended.

Disillusion with the treaty was not limited to Germany and the United

World War I officially ended with the signing of the Treaty of Versailles in the Hall of Mirrors on June 28, 1919.

From the League to the United Nations

Although the United States rejected the Treaty of Versailles and did not join the League of Nations, Woodrow Wilson's dream of founding an international body to settle disputes between nations lived on after him. The idea was not his alone. The British foreign secretary Sir Edward Grey advocated the establishment of such an organization, and earlier political philosophers dreamed of a way to end the long history of warfare between nations.

The League of Nations ultimately failed to stop the increasing aggression of the 1930s. It took another world war to convince the world that such a body was in the common interest. Discredited, the league lingered on until 1946. But a new organization, the United Nations, had begun to facilitate international security after its founding in October 1945. Today, the United Nations plays an active role in settling international disputes around the globe.

States. The British felt that the treaty was unfair to Germany, especially the war reparations that were determined after the treaty was signed. In the coming years, the Germans would start to ignore the restrictions placed on their military and condemn the treaty outright. "Between the retreat of America and the treacheries of Europe the Treaties of Peace were never given a fair trial,"[65]

wrote British prime minister David Lloyd George, who had negotiated on behalf of Great Britain.

Archibald Wavell, a British officer who fought in both world wars, felt that the treaty terms contributed to postwar fighting and to the outbreak of the Second World War. "After the 'war to end war,'" he wrote, "they seem to have been pretty successful in Paris at making a 'Peace to end Peace.'"[66]

Notes

Introduction: The Reason Why

1. Quoted in Patrick Glynn, *Closing Pandora's Box: Arms Races, Arms Control, and the History of the Cold War*. New York: Basic, 1992, p. 3.
2. Glynn, *Closing Pandora's Box,* p. 41.
3. Quoted in Philip Magnus, *King Edward VII*. New York: Penguin, 1979, p. 269.
4. Quoted in Magnus, *King Edward VII,* p. 513.
5. Winston S. Churchill, *The World Crisis*. New York: Scribner's, 1931, p. 6.
6. Quoted in Brian Gardner, ed., *Up the Line to Death: The War Poets, 1914–1918*. London: Methuen, 1964, p. 127.

Chapter One: The Western Front—the Center of the Storm

7. Quoted in Barbara W. Tuchman, *The Guns of August*. New York: Ballantine, 1994, p. 119.
8. Quoted in Louis Raemaekers, *Raemaekers' Cartoon History of the War*, vol. 1. New York: Century, 1919, p. 8.
9. Quoted in Raemaekers, *Raemaekers' Cartoon History of the War,* p. 10.
10. Churchill, *The World Crisis,* p. 11.
11. Marshal Foch, *The Memoirs of Marshal Foch*. Garden City, NY: Doubleday, Doran, 1931, p. 35.
12. Foch, *The Memoirs of Marshal Foch,* p. 117.

13. Quoted in John J. Pershing, *My Experiences in the World War*, vol. 1. New York: Stokes, 1931, p. 166.

Chapter Two: War on the Sea and in the Air

14. Churchill, *The World Crisis,* p. 85.
15. Quoted in Britain & Germany: The Naval Arms Race, "Britain's Policy as Outlined in the Speech in Parliament of the Foreign Secretary, Sir Edward Grey: March 29, 1909." http://web.jjay.cuny.edu/~jobrien/reference/ob71.html.
16. Quoted in Geoffrey Parker, ed., *The Cambridge Illustrated History of Warfare*. New York: Cambridge University Press, p. 283.
17. Quoted in Cyril Falls, *The Great War*. New York: Putnam's Sons, 1959, p. 212.
18. Churchill, *The World Crisis,* p. 310.

Chapter Three: War in the Near East

19. Churchill, *The World Crisis,* p. 325.
20. Quoted in Churchill, *The World Crisis,* p. 325.
21. Ellis Ashmead-Bartlett, "*The Sydney Morning Herald*, May 8, 1915," National Library of Australia. www.nla.gov.au/gallipolidespatches/2–2-3-ashmead.html.
22. Quoted in Gardner, *Up the Line to Death,* p. 60.

23. Archibald P. Wavell, *The Palestine Campaigns*. Freeport, NY: Books for Libraries, 1972, p. 21.

24. Quoted in Parker, *The Cambridge Illustrated History of Warfare*, p. 276.

25. Quoted in Byron Farwell, *Armies of the Raj: From the Great Indian Mutiny to Independence, 1858–1947*. New York: Norton, 1991, p. 261.

26. Wavell, *The Palestine Campaigns*, p. 15.

27. Wavell, *The Palestine Campaigns*, p. 14.

28. T.E. Lawrence, *Seven Pillars of Wisdom*. Garden City, New York: International Collectors Library, 1938, p. 64.

29. Lawrence, *Seven Pillars of Wisdom*, p. 74.

30. Lawrence, *Seven Pillars of Wisdom*, p. 186.

31. Lawrence, *Seven Pillars of Wisdom*, p. 165.

32. Lawrence, *Seven Pillars of Wisdom*, p. 277.

33. Wavell, *The Palestine Campaigns*, p. 167.

Chapter Four: War on the Eastern Front—The Old WorldCrumbles

34. Quoted in Parker, *The Cambridge Illustrated History of Warfare*, p. 274.

35. Falls, *The Great War*, p. 220.

36. John Reed, *Ten Days That Shook the World*. New York: Random House, 1960, p. 8.

37. Reed, *Ten Days That Shook the World*, p. 10.

38. Quoted in Reed, *Ten Days That Shook the World*, p. 26.

39. Quoted in David Robin Watson, *Georges Clemenceau: A Political Biography*. New York: David McKay, 1974, p. 298.

Chapter Five: America on the March

40. Quoted in John Keegan, *The First World War*. New York: Knopf, 1999, p. 50.

41. Quoted in University of Virginia Library, http://etext.virginia.edu/jefferson/quotations/jeff1400.htm.

42. Quoted in Henry F. Pringle, *Theodore Roosevelt*. New York: Harcourt, Brace, Jovanovich, 1984, p. 408.

43. Quoted in Barbara Tuchman, *The Zimmermann Telegram*. New York: Macmillan, 1966, p. 176.

44. Tuchman, *The Zimmermann Telegram*, pp. 176–77.

45. Pershing, *My Experiences in the World War*, p. 102.

46. Foch, *The Memoirs of Marshal Foch*, p. 346.

47. Quoted in Byron Farwell, *Over There: The United States in the Great War, 1917–1918*. New York: Norton, 1999, p. 106.

48. Quoted in Farwell, *Over There*, p. 19.

49. Foch, *The Memoirs of Marshal Foch*, p. 368.

50. Pershing, *My Experiences in the World War*, p. 162.

51. Quoted in Farwell, *Over There*, p. 228.

52. Foch, *The Memoirs of Marshal Foch*, p. 387.

53. Quoted in Watson, *Georges Clemenceau*, p. 325.

Chapter Six: Versailles and After

54. Quoted in History Matters, "Making the World 'Safe for Democracy': Woodrow Wilson Asks for War." http://historymatters.gmu.edu/d/4943/.

55. Quoted in Margaret MacMillan, *Paris 1919: Six Months That Changed the World*. New York: Random House, 2002, p. 495.

56. Quoted in Valerie Pakenham, *Out in the Noonday Sun: Edwardians in the Tropics*. New York: Random House, 1985, p. 218.

57. Quoted in MacMillan, *Paris 1919*, p. 495.

58. Quoted in John Bagot Glubb, *Britain and the Arabs: A Study of Fifty Years, 1908 to 1958*. London: Hodder and Stoughton, 1959, p. 74.

59. Quoted in Malcolm Brown, *Lawrence of Arabia: The Life, the Legend*. New York: Thames and Hudson, 2005, p. 145.

60. Quoted in Robert Lansing, *The Peace Negotiations: A Personal Narrative*. Port Washington, NY: Kennikat, 1921, pp. 260–61.

61. Lansing, *The Peace Negotiations*, p. 263.

62. Quoted in André Tardieu, *The Truth About the Treaty*. Indianapolis, IN: Bobbs-Merrill, 1921, p. 184.

63. Quoted in MacMillan, *Paris 1919*, p. 192.

64. Quoted in MacMillan, *Paris 1919*, p. 476.

65. David Lloyd George, *Memoirs of the Peace Conference*, vol. 2. New Haven, CT: Yale University Press, 1939, p. 914.

66. Quoted in David Fromkin, *A Peace to End All Peace*. New York: Henry Holt, 1989, p. 5.

For More Information

Books

Simon Adams, *World War I.* New York: DK, 2001. This well-illustrated overview of the First World War includes exhibitions and photos from London's Imperial War Museum.

Peter I. Bosco and Antoinette Bosco, *World War I: America at War.* New York: Facts On File, 2003. A short history of America's involvement in World War I.

Malcolm Brown, *Lawrence of Arabia: The Life, the Legend.* New York: Thames and Hudson, 2005. This heavily illustrated book provides a good introduction to the exploits of the British officer who led Arab tribes in a revolt against the Ottoman Turks during World War I.

Neil Champion, *Poets of the First World War.* Oxford, UK: Heinemann Educational Books, 2003. A good introduction to the writings of soldiers in World War I.

Franz Coetzee and Marilyn Shervin-Coetzee, *World War I: A History in Documents.* New York: Oxford University Press, 2002. A useful resource for primary documents on the First World War.

Giles Foden, Mimi *and* Toutou's *Big Adventure: The Bizarre Battle of Lake Tanganyika.* New York: Vintage, 2004. A humorous retelling of the clashes between Allied and German forces in Africa.

R.G. Grant, *How Did It Happen? World War I.* San Diego: Lucent, 2005. A closer look at some of the factors in the outbreak of war in 1914.

Jeff Hay, ed., *At Issue in History: The Treaty of Versailles.* Chicago: Greenhaven, 2001. An examination through a series of articles of the treaty that officially ended World War I.

Adam Hibbert, *In the Trenches in World War I.* Oxford, UK: Raintree, 2006. A closer look at life at war on the western front.

John Keegan, *An Illustrated History of the First World War.* New York: Knopf, 2001. This single-volume history by a noted British historian provides an overview of the war and includes numerous pictures.

Walter Dean Myers and Bill Miles, *The Harlem Hellfighters: When Pride Met Courage.* New York: HarperCollins, 2006. A well-illustrated history of New York's African American regiment that fought in France during World War I.

Earle Rice Jr., *World War I Flying Aces.* San Diego: Lucent, 2002. A look at America's earliest fighter pilots and their role in World War I.

The Smithsonian Institution, *Legend, Memory and the Great War in the Air.* Seattle: University of Washington Press, 1992. This well-illustrated book produced by the Smithsonian's National Air and Space Museum traces the rise in the popular imagination of the fighter ace in World War I and its subsequent imprint on popular culture.

Karen Zeinert, *Those Extraordinary Women of World War I*. Brookfield, CT: Millbrook, 2001. A history of the contribution of women to the war effort and the social changes that resulted.

Films

All Quiet on the Western Front (1930). Universal Studios Home Video. A film adaptation of the novel by Erich Maria Remarque about life in the German trenches on the European front. The author was a German veteran of the Great War.

Blackadder Goes Forth (1983–1989). BBC series. This British comedic series represents the wry wit of the Tommy, or common British soldier, as he attempts to cope with the absurdities of life on the western front.

Gallipoli (1981). Paramount Home Entertainment. Australian units of the Allied forces participate in the failed attempt to force the Dardanelles and knock Turkey out of the war.

Hell's Angels (1930). Universal Studios Home Video. American movie mogul Howard Hughes produced a vivid representation of WWI aerial combat in this 1930 film. It follows the adventures of two brothers who join the Royal Flying Corps at the outbreak of World War I.

Lawrence of Arabia (1962). Columbia Studios. T.E. Lawrence, an eccentric British officer, organizes resistance to Ottoman Turkish rule in the Middle East. The film captures the mobility of desert warfare—a stark contrast to the static trench warfare of the western

front—and touches on the problem of nationalist aspirations in Arab lands resulting from Allied wartime promises to their Arab allies.

The Lost Battalion (2001). A&E Network Studios. This televised film captures the harrowing experiences of American soldiers cut off in the Argonne Forest in 1918. The forces were vastly outnumbered by Germans, but refused to surrender or retreat.

Web Sites

BBC, World War I (www.bbc.co.uk/schools/worldwarone/). An excellent interactive site by the British Broadcasting Corporation about World War I, featuring animation, games, and contemporary stories.

First World War.com (www.firstworldwar.com/index.htm). An online World War I resource that includes lots of pictures and many interesting short articles.

The History Department at the United States Military Academy, World War I (www.dean.usma.edu/history/web03/atlases/great%20war/great%20war%20index.htm). A selection of detailed color maps of World War I battlefields presented by the U.S. Military Academy at West Point.

Imperial War Museum (www.iwm.org.uk/). The Web site of London's Imperial War Museum, which features online exhibitions, reference material, and photographs about World War I.

SchoolHistory.co.uk (www.schoolhistory.co.uk/lessons/wwi/objectives_wwi.html). This British Web site tests your knowledge of the causes of World War I through an interactive quiz.

Index

Picture Credits

About the Author

Robert Green is a regular contributor to Economist Intelligence Unit publications on East Asia and a former employee of the Government Information Office of the Republic of China. He holds a master's degree in journalism from New York University and a master's degree in area studies from Harvard University. He has been interested in the history of the First World War for many years. This is his thirty-first book for students.